NORWAY

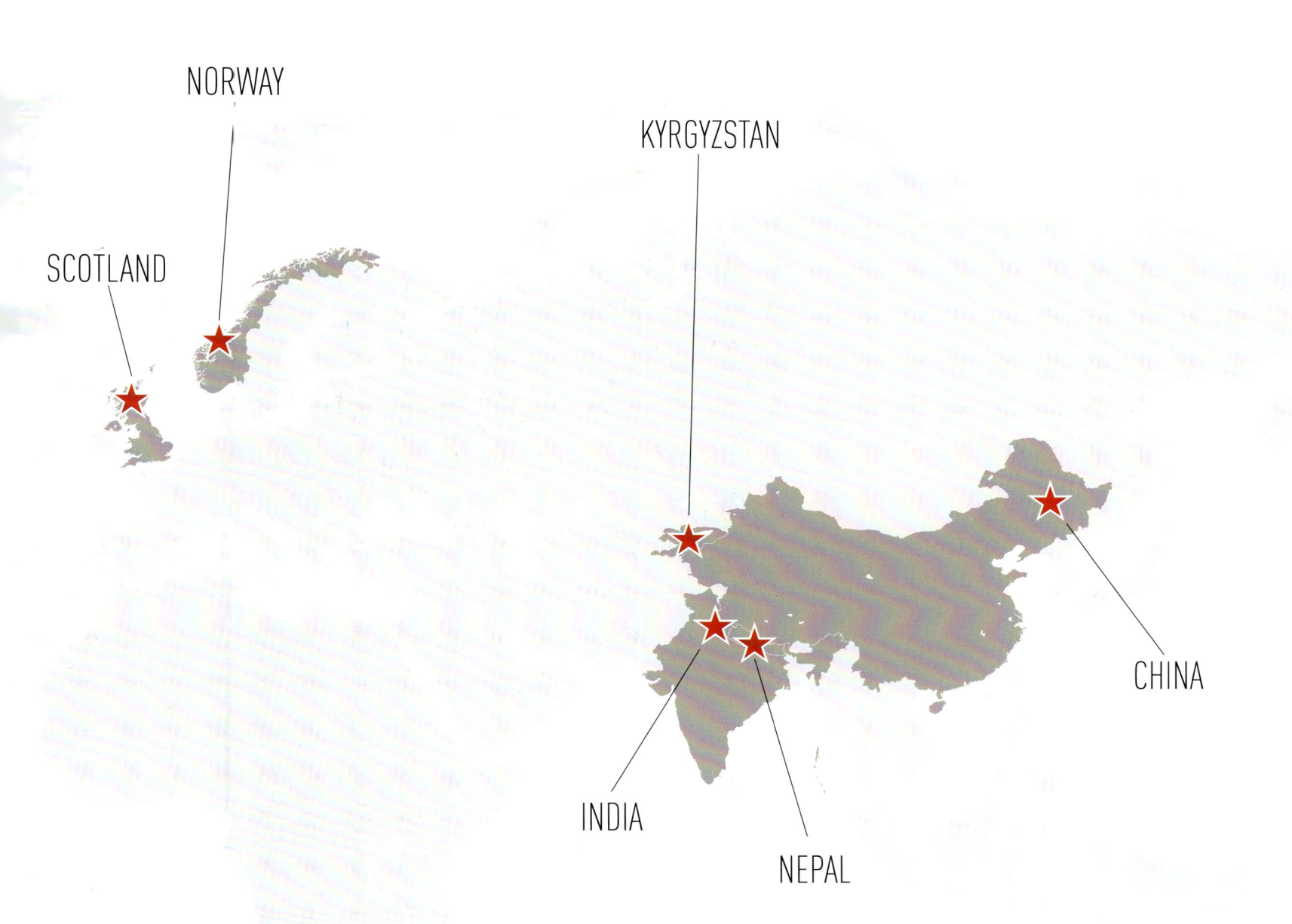

KYRGYZSTAN

SCOTLAND

★

★

CHINA

★

★ ★

INDIA

NEPAL

Chamonix, Argentière glacier.

CONTENT

ADVANCEMENT	ADVENTURE 2000 – 2012	10
INDIA	ARWA TOWER 2007	28
CANADA	ICEFALL BROOK CANYON 2008	36
NEPAL	KWANGDE SHAR 2008/2009	50
CANADA	CIRQUE OF THE UNCLIMBABLES 2009	66
SCOTLAND	ROADTRIP 2010/2011	78
FRIENDS	COMPANIONS	90
KYRGYZSTAN I	KYZYL ASKER 2010	98
KYRGYZSTAN II	KYZYL ASKER 2011	114
CHINA	HARBIN 2012	118
NORWAY	ROMSDALEN 2012	128
ARCTIC	BAFFIN ISLAND	MOUNT ASGARD 2012	140

INES PAPERT

I LOVE THE variety of my passion. Whether it's rock or mountain climbing, in the ice or on a cliff, by creating my own in the high mountains of the Himalayas, or indeed climbing on my doorstep, on domestic cliffs – the mountains mean nearly everything to me. I've been able to experience the meaning, and learned to adapt and adjust to the situations that are waiting for me in foreign regions.

I am not interested in getting »higher, faster, further« or breaking any records. In fact, it's the style of the ascent that stimulates me. With a light backpack, with a small team, quickly reaching the peak and getting back down again – before the weather turns for the worse – this is what I am looking for. Climbing the alpine style way. That means, to a great extent climbing without bolts and static ropes, not leaving any clips behind. That includes also, taking into consideration uncomfortable bivvies in exposed locations and to know at the finish, that at every point in time, I gave everything. For me, less desirable is the thought of spending weeks camped beside a face or mountain, waiting for ideal conditions, because a strategic move might work out. I know exactly what my limits are. I prepare myself well for every venture, meticulously calculating the risks and listening to my inner voice. Success and failure in the mountains lie very close to one another. Failing to reach the summits hurts, yet it is not the end of the world. Thanks to my persistence, I don't give in easily and keep trying, again and again.

On an expedition, I can find my inner peace and unlike everyday life, I can completely concentrate and focus on my objectives. I can live and be my very own self.

The challenges that I set for myself in the mountains as a very determined person, give me the necessary balance to my life. My biggest assignment is being a Mother. My son Emanuel means a lot more to me than the mountains. He means everything to me. My son gives me the strength that I need to reach my goals, and to cope with the ups and downs that you have when you are on the mountains. On our travels together in foreign countries, when sleeping out in the open, my son and I experience freedom. A freedom that I missed during my childhood and youth, being confined within the Soviet occupied zone of the GDR. We had to fight for our freedom and we eventually got it. Today, my home is the Berchtesgadener Land. I have found happiness in the steep walls of the world. I feel privileged to be able to make a living from my passion as a professional mountain climber and I am very grateful.

With this illustrated book, I wish to share with you my experiences. Maybe, with this book, I can encourage people to go forward. It is never too late to fulfill one's dreams. All that is needed is a conscious decision.

Ines Papert

ADVANCEMENT & ADVENTURE

»Haugsfossen« WI6 in Norway, Rjukan.

ICE IS A MEDIUM that I thoroughly enjoy. With ice, I have so much to be grateful for. In 1999, I took time off from my profession – I worked as a physiotherapist – to commit myself to a whole year of climbing. At that time, I did not predict, that it would be the final farewell to the professional life that I knew. Like so often in my life, everything worked out differently. I became pregnant. In 2000, my son Manu was born. This meant that I could no longer go on long trips. Hence, I started looking for an alternative, where I could be a good mother to my son and still pursue my great passion. The newly founded ce climbing World Cup allowed me to combine both desires. Without any great expectations, I travelled to the first events. During my six year involvement with the World Cup series, I was able to win four World Championships, 13 single World Cups and the overall World Cup Series three times. I always brought my little baby Manu with me to the weekend competitions. I was a very happy mother and a successful sportswoman. Suddenly, I was able to support myself with prize money and sponsorship agreements.

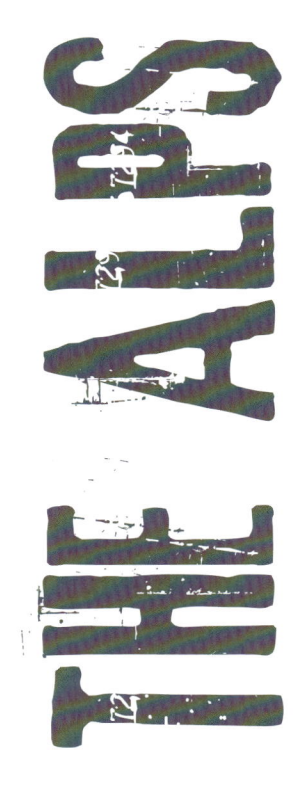

MISSION IMPOSSIBLE | M11 | REDPOINT
VALSAVARENCHE/ITALY 2003
GEAR: NORMAL PITONS AND ICE SCREWS

THE ALPS

I ONCE SUCCESSFULLY participated in the Ouray Ice Festival (USA), taking first place in the overall standings of both ladies' and mens' categories, this was the highlight of my competitive career and at the time, I was thinking of getting out then and there. It's best to quit when you are at the top. Apart from this, I didn't want to define myself any further through rivalry and competition. I wanted to go back to my roots, where everything began: to the mountains, the Alps. After I succeeded repeating the route called »Mission Impossible« (M11) in the Aosta valley, which was then regarded as the most difficult mixed route, my decision was made.

In 2008, under ideal conditions on the Breitwangfluh in Bernese Oberland, I climbed the route »Flying Circus« (M10) on-sight, exactly ten years to the day Robert Jasper had achieved the very first ascent.

»I have been waiting for many years for good conditions in ›The Flying Circus‹. At last I stand under this spectacular and awesome face.« *Ines Papert*

THE FLYING CIRCUS | M10 | ONSIGHT

HEIGHT OF FACE: 140 M

GEAR: SEVERAL PITONS, BOLTED BELAYS, ICE SCREWS

NORTH FACES

EIGER NORTH FACE

SYMPHONIE DE LIBERTÉ 8A REDPOINT
HEIGHT OF FACE: 900 M

NOT ONLY DO I enjoy myself on ice, I also enjoy cliffs. I am particularly fond of north faces. I like the exposure, the steepness and the cool temperatures.
My first long alpine route, where I took part with a team, including Hans Lochner, where we were able to climb redpoint, was the »Symphonie de Liberté« (8a) at the Genfer Pfeiler (Geneva pillar) on the Eiger north face. I had a bad accident on the Marmolada south face in 2005, during the route called »The track through the fish« a rock scale became loose, which ended in me having a nasty fall. During the cumbersome rehabilitation, I was able to motivate myself to start thinking and planning one of my projects on the Tre Cime di Lavaredo. The redpoint ascent »Camilotto Pellisier« (8a+), is the most difficult route on the north face of the big peak. »Bubu« Mauro Bole was the first person, back in 2004, to do the free climb.

2003 with Hans Lochner in 14 hours redpoint to the peak of the Genfer Pfeiler (Geneva pillar). Bernese Oberland/Switzerland.

VIA CAMILOTTO PELLISIER | 8A+/8B

HEIGHT OF FACE: 600 M

GEAR: 6 MM BOLTS BOLTED BELAYS

DOLOMITES/ITALY 2006

TODAY, THE ALPS offer me unlimited worthwhile destinations. I call this the »playground«, on my doorstep. When Manu was still small and I wasn't able to go away on long expeditions, I spent most of the time on the local mountains. I love the Alps. It's a love that will never end. Even when I travel once or twice a year, to go on expeditions off the beaten track, searching for my goals, I love returning, back to the large walls of the Alps. This is where I feel »at home«.

»John Avarette showing us in ›King Cat‹ 5.11+/Indian Creek the technique of crack climbing.« *Ines Papert*

UTAH

SCARFACE | 5.11- | INDIAN CREEK

INDIAN CREEK IS a true paradise. If you want to learn crack climbing, this is the place to train. The friction of the red sandstone is ideal, to get closer and understand traditional climbing. For me, the trip to Utah was a mixture of a tour and a holiday with my son, combined with the sport that I love: Climbing. This was my first large venture together with Manu, who was five years old at the time. My last big journey with Hari Berger. I knew Hari very well from the time we spent competing in tournaments. We had a very close, friendly relationship with one another and we decided, after spending time together in winter in Norway, that we would set out together in the summer. Six weeks of wild camping, in the middle of nowhere, at the same time, climbing until the fingers bleed – those were the days, Hari!

»Fine Jade« 5.11- The Rectory, Desert Towers.

Hari Berger successfully conquers the red point ascent of Pink Flamingo, 5.13.

HARI was the complete motivation machine. Tackling a route like the »Pink Flamingo«, he could handle the torture like nobody else. He would get up around 5 am, as conditions at that time of the morning, were ideal. That was no problem for Hari, although I had problems getting up at that time. Luckily, we got to know several very friendly local people, who supported us, either serving as safety partners, taking care of Manu while I was climbing. My son was fully integrated and part of a large and somewhat crazy family.

Hari undertook the trip with me and Manu, seeing it as a test run. At that time, he was in a relationship with Kirsten. Both of them were seriously considering starting a family. Hari wanted to see if he could combine his desire to have children with his passion for climbing. Manu loved Hari, his buddy. Our time in Utah was hilarious, carefree, and for Hari very convincing. His girlfriend Kirsten became pregnant shortly afterwards. Baby Zoe was born in December 2006, just a few hours after Hari lost his life when an ice grotto collapsed at Hintersee. Hari, I know you would be very proud of your two girls, Kirsten und Zoe. I also know that you are reading this page: You were truly a great friend. We sorely miss you.

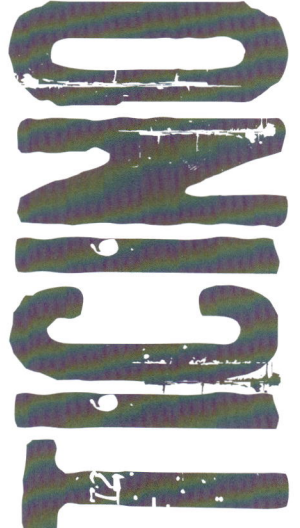

TICINO

TRADITIONAL CLIMBING IN TICINO (SWITZERLAND). The route »Super Cirill« (8a/8a+) which lies in the Valle di Bavona is the most difficult free climbing multi-pitch route in Ticino. Together with my friend, World Champion climber Liv Sanzos from France, we tried the route back in 2010. Tropical temperatures and violent thunderstorms prevented us from getting through the final passage. One year later, Liv couldn't take part. I ended up completing the redpoint route with Charly Fritzer. One of the most beautiful routes I have ever climbed.

Granite in Ticino
»Together with Liv Sanzos, I worked on the crux on ›Super Cirill‹ 8a(+) the 11-pitches-route in Valle di Bavona. I make it through the passage after many attempts, a year later. Among the finest crack climbs.« *Ines Papert*

DOLOMITES

»**ILLUMINATI**« (M11+) in Langental near Wolkenstein demands not only skill but also patience. »Illuminati« takes its time letting people climb up. Only then, when there is enough ice on the upper part of the face, can the mixed route be climbed. Only then, is the free standing ice pillar connected to the rock shelter below. Since Albert Leichtfried first climbed »Illuminati« in 2006, I toyed with the idea of following him up and I undertook several attempts. Sometimes there wasn't enough ice and sometimes the temperatures were too low. To successfully climb this rarity, everything has to be perfect. Including the network. In January 2012 – I was hardly back from Harbin, China – when I got a phone call from Hubert Moroder, a good friend and mountain guide from St. Ulrich: »Ines, you have to come! Immediately!« Included in the team was once again my old friend Lisi Steurer. By the way, Hubert wasn't just our informant; he was also our caring hostel warden. In the Lastei residence, Lisi and I were totally spoiled. I managed the rock ceiling straight away. For safety reasons, we only tackled the stretch of ice that followed after the sun had disappeared behind the mountain. I became queasy when I stood in front of the metre long column. A freestanding 20 metre high ice column can be fragile and very dangerous. If it collapses, it will drag you down very deep. That's why we decided not to set any ice bolts into the column. Instead we positioned the next safety device further up, where the ice merges into the cliff. My thoughts were spine-chilling.

No bolts in vertical climbing at 20 metres! If you fall, it hits you unsecured at the front end. Then I had a good feeling, as the temperature was around zero degrees and this helped reduce the dangerous tension. I climbed with Lisi up to the exit. We couldn't help screaming our joy. I was able to repeat the »Illuminati« redpoint and Lisi had just successfully completed her degree exams a few days earlier. We had every reason to celebrate this evening.

»I capture Albert Leichtfried's ›Illuminati‹ M11/WI6+ at Langental redpoint. My friend Lisi Steurer is there helping me.« *Ines Papert*

INDIA
ARWA TOWER

garhwal

MY FIRST GREAT expedition takes me to the Indian part of the Himalayas. The Garhwal is not just breathtakingly beautiful, it is also a highly spiritual region. The divine mountains are visited by pilgrims from all over India. Apart from that, framed by peaks between six and seven thousand metres high, the holy source of the Ganges River arises from here. Religion and nature are impressively interconnected with each other in Garhwal. The 6.352 metre high Arwa Tower will teach and shape me.

MY FRIENDS Stephan Siegrist, Denis Burdet and Thomas Senf have the high aim of being the first to climb the north face of the Arwa Tower. I am grateful that they are taking me with them. Being relatively inexperienced in large expeditions, not only do I join their project, I also follow my own aim: Repeating the French route through the west pillar. Yet I also gain a lot from the alpine experience and logistics of the accurate Swiss team members. In the run up, there is little for me to take care of. My expedition is supposed to be like a type of trial lesson. It later develops into a dramatic crash course in expedition mountaineering. A Swiss girl, Anita Kolar, who was 18 years-old at the time, will form a close friendship with me.

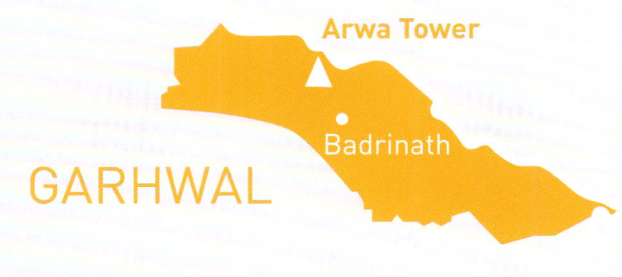

WILD GARHWAL

FROM DELHI ONWARDS, we spend days on a bus driving on bumpy roads via Rishikesh and Joshimath, heading for Badrinath. From there, we are accompanied by carriers and a cook up to the 4.350 metre high base camp. I am the cook's favourite, being the only one able to eat normally. All of the others are having problems with diarrhea and are eating plain rice instead. Although the three chaps are able to recover swiftly, Anita appears to be getting worse. She also suffers from headaches.

Anita and I trained together in the run up to this tour on the Großglockner. There I already felt the amount of pressure Anita was putting herself under. It was the same here, on the way to the base camp. Although Anita wasn't at her physical best, she kept pace courageously. Her motivation and ambition for an 18-year-old is remarkable. However, she covered up her weakness. When we arrived at the base camp, she collapsed in her tent, hardly reacting when we spoke to her. She was coughing non-stop, rattling. Her condition was getting worse by the minute. We all knew immediately, what this means. She had to be taken down – straight away. The men made a sledge from a haulbag. In a six hour, energy-sapping nighttime operation, we pulled and carried Anita to an empty

military installation in Gastoli. The appropriate medicine and the lower altitude worked,, thank God. The following morning, she could come down with me to Badrinath and then take the bus down the valley to Joshimath. There she was able to spend a few days in the hotel recovering. On my way back up to the base camp, I can't stop thinking whether we will still have the time to try climbing the face. My impatience is completely out of place. Particularly up in the high mountains. I am satisfied that we were able to help Anita. That is what really matters.

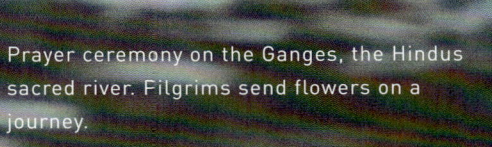

Prayer ceremony on the Ganges, the Hindus sacred river. Pilgrims send flowers on a journey.

»Snow and ice prevent us from making progress. The weather starts to change.« *Ines Papert*

Transport of material to the advanced base camp.

PILIER GUILHEM CHAFFIOL | 6B/M7
NORTH WEST COLUMN | HEIGHT OF FACE: 600 M
ALPINE STYLE | WE'RE ONLY 200 M AWAY FROM THE SUMMIT | 1 BIVVY

POSITION: 30°50'36''N 79°23'03''E

AFTER A FEW DAYS, Anita makes it back to us. Of course she is feeble and somewhat groggy. Yet she has made a reasonable recovery. We light up, telling each other jokes, fooling around, laughing and experience a lot of joy. The incident, although being very dramatic, did our team some good. It welded us together. One for all. We've learned a lesson. It's the team that makes you strong, not the ego. Sometimes that even weakens you.

Anita and I eventually dare a single attempt at the west face and we complete two-thirds of the route before the weather changes. I have to admit that I don't find the upcoming storm inconvenient. We abandon and return back to the camp. Taking responsibility for Anita is too big a risk. I am not yet prepared for this situation. By the way, in Sanskrit, Arwa means »horse«. It didn't want to tame both of us – »Expedition-Greenhorns« yet. Also Stephan, Denis and Thomas have a fight on their hands, before they succeed in the first ascent of the route »Lightning Strike«, they spend a whole twelve days on the face.

CANADA
ICEFALL BROOK CANYON

»A dream comes true! In this wild countryside of the Canadian Rockies, up to 600 metre waterfalls in gorges freeze into ice. Very few less difficult routes have been climbed before we arrived.« *Ines Papert*

THE ISOLATED CANYON »Icefall Brook« in British Columbia is a huge amphitheatre composing of rocks, ice and snow. This area is practically unexplored.

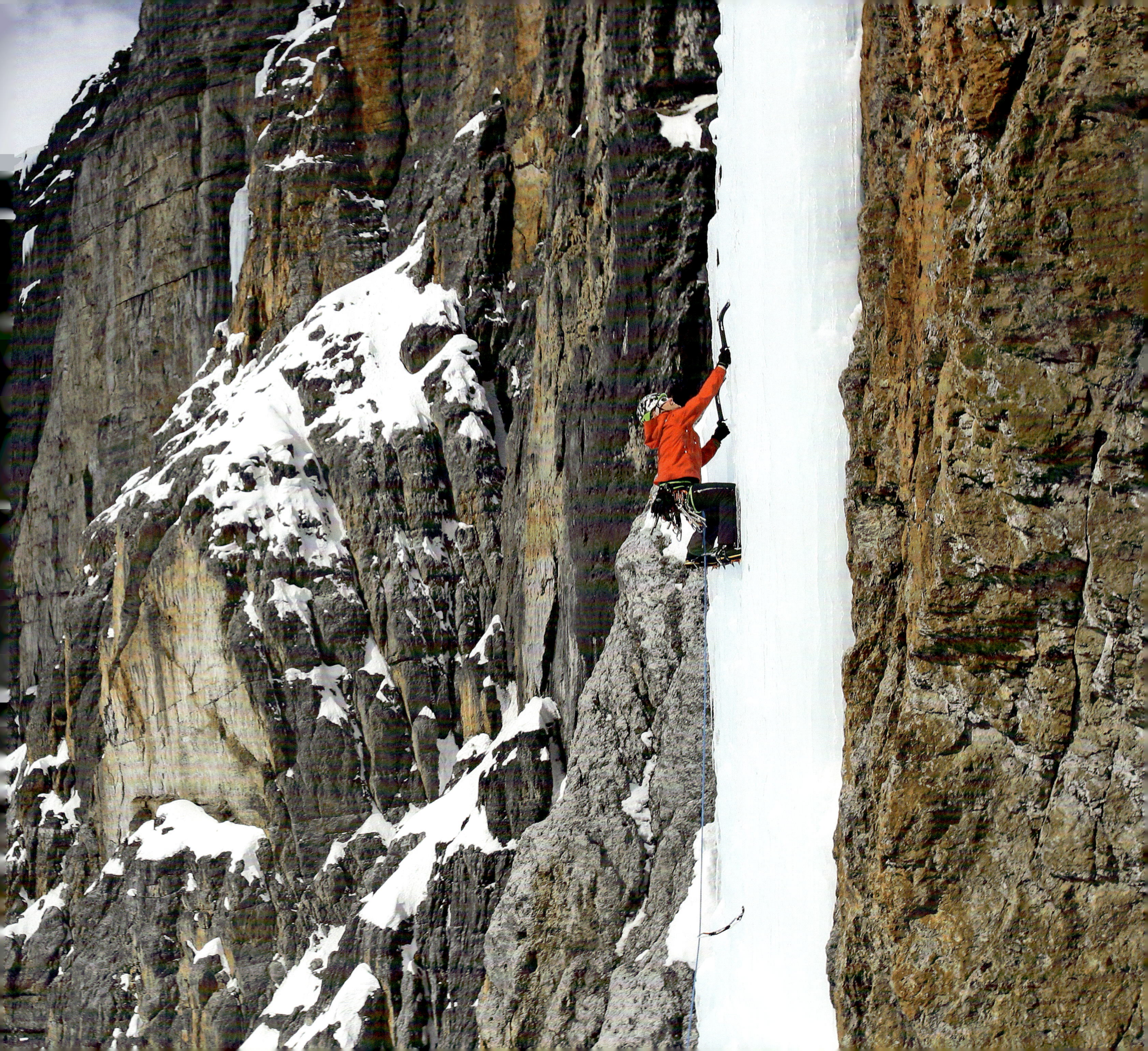

CANADA

Icefall Brook Canyon
Golden • Calgary

DURING A SKI crossing through the Rocky Mountains, my pal Jon Walsh, an ice climber and photographer, discovers this wild canyon. After showing me his pictures, we decide together with Audrey Gariepy, Jennifer Olson and Caroline George to head for this region to explore the area. The canyon is isolated and, due to the danger of avalanches in winter it's almost unreachable. We buy so much food in Golden, it heats up the credit card. This is mainly due to the fact that we'll be flying there by helicopter. Because of the precarious avalanche situation, we cannot travel there on our own – it's too risky.

RECIPE
»BACKCOUNTRY ICE CREAM«

1 LITRE (!) OF BAILEYS
1 LITRE OF CREAM

ADDITIONALLY STIR WITH LOTS OF FRESH POWDER SNOW, THEN LET FREEZE AND THAT'S IT! ONLY POSSIBLE WITH CANADIAN POWDER SNOW, DUE TO THE FACT IT'S WONDERFULLY DRY AND FLUFFY.

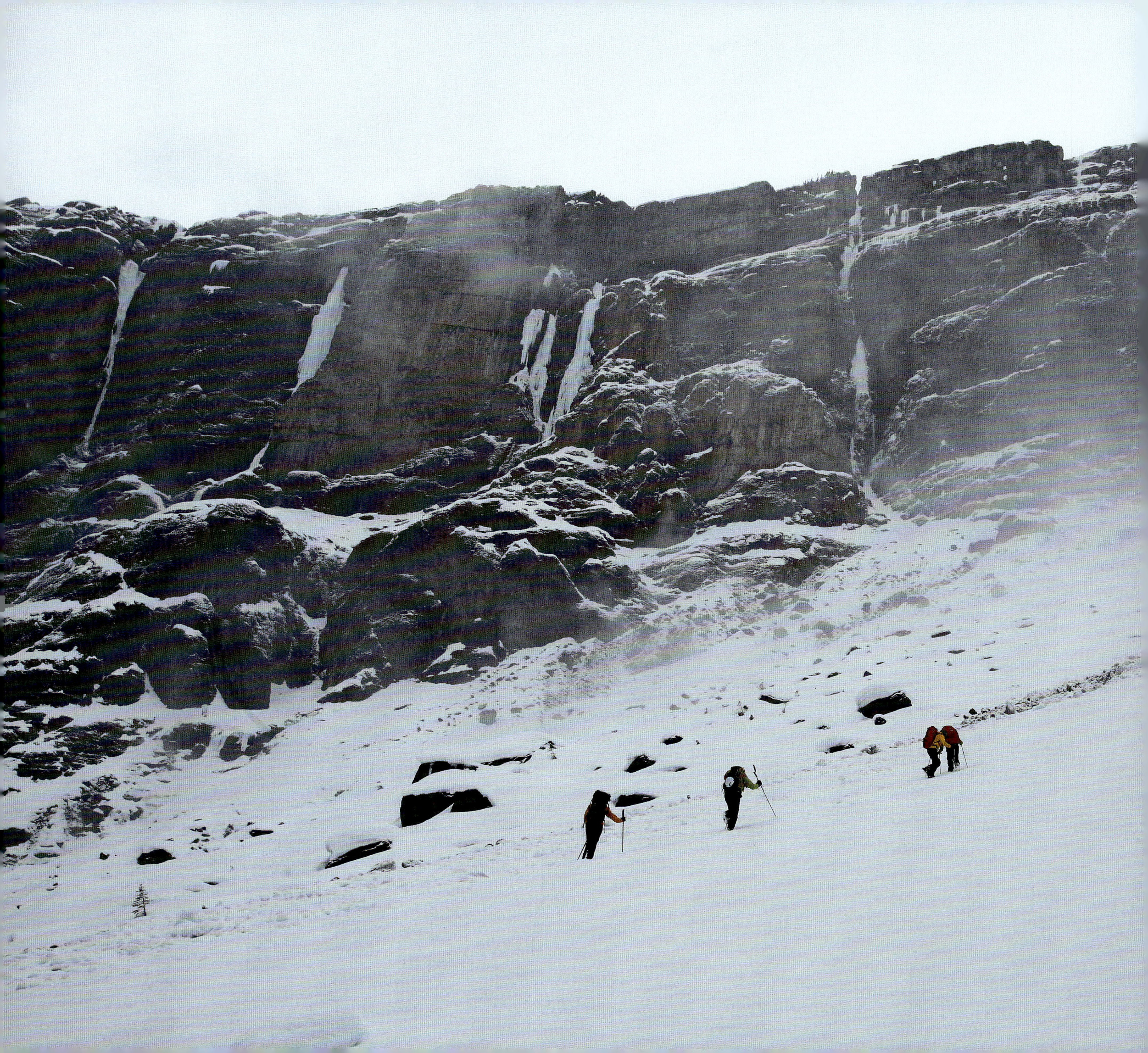

»It's not easy making the decision. Where should we begin? There are so many possibilities.« *Ines Papert*

FOUR GIRLS AND a photographer in the wilderness! Cut off from the outside world. At nighttime, we are kept awake from the howling of the wolves. We are expecting up to 600 metre long unspoiled ice paths and mixed routes. The access paths are comparatively simple. The conditions are very good: an overcast sky, occasional snow fall, ideal temperatures slightly below freezing point. We are able to take advantage of the daylight.

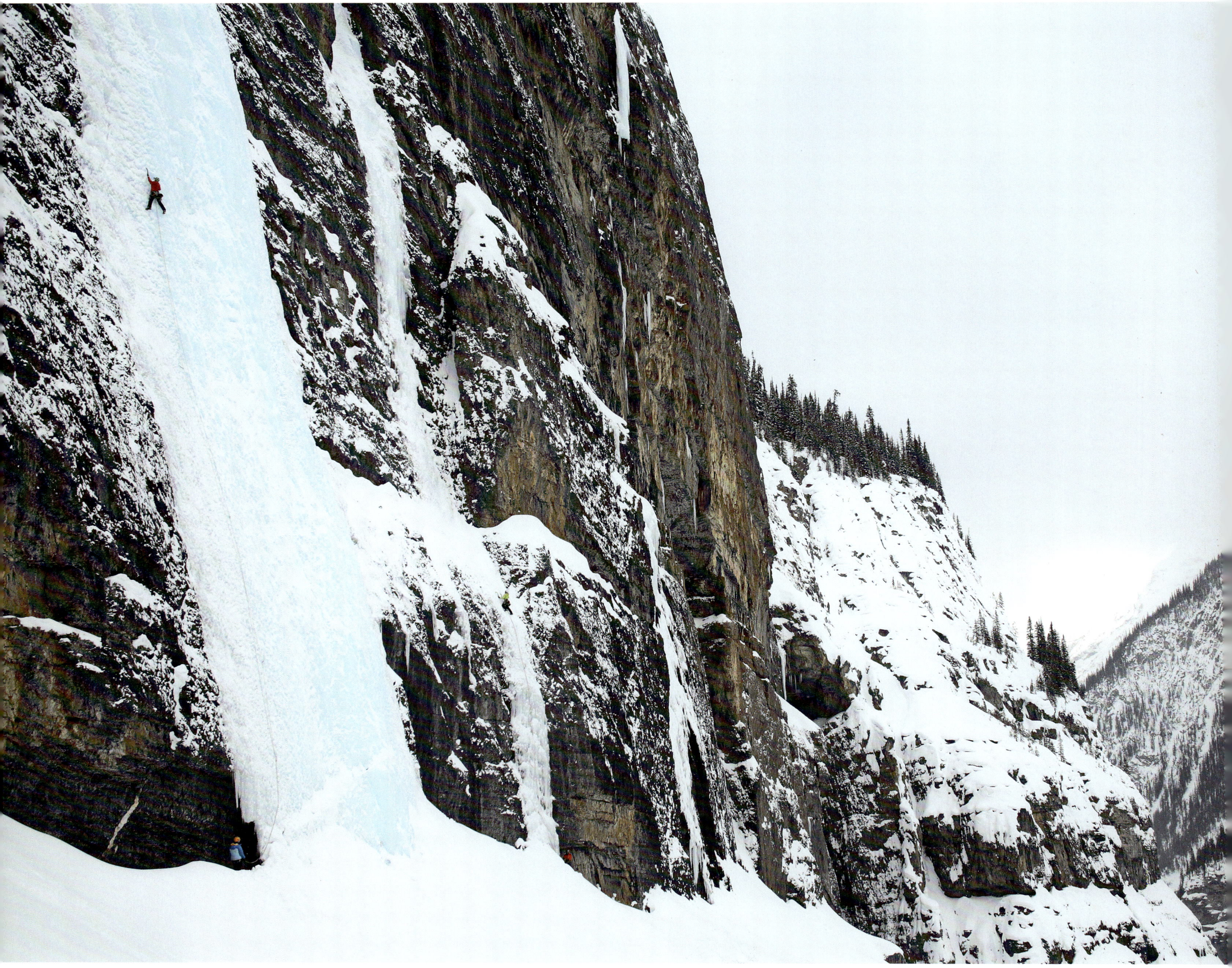

FIRST ASCENTS:

HAPPY BIRTHDAY	WI5	120 M
BLUE LAGOON	WI5	200 M
HIGH FIVE	WI5+	200 M
NORTHWEST PASSAGE	WI5+	600 M
KEEP ON SMILING	WI6	60 M
FOSSEN FALLS	WI6	170 M
HAPPY HOURS	WI6	240 M
JUSQU'AU BOUT	M5/WI6	200 M
SUPERNATURAL B.C.	M7/WI6	600 M

AUDREY AND I form a team of two. Caroline and Jen do the same. None of the days go to waste. We manage a total of ten first ascents in ten days, including the »Northwest Passage« (WI5, 600 metres), »Scrambled Pancakes« (M7/WI6, 600 metres) and »Happy Hours« (WI6, 300 metres) with a terrific deep view. In the evenings, we get closer together in our kitchen tent, cooking and chatting with each other. We feel satisfied with what we have achieved so far. However, one route that came to my attention just won't leave my mind. A huge cave high up one of the faces with a fine formation of ice above it.

INTO THE WILD

»I am physically and mentally exhausted, yet having this goal in front of my eyes gives me an enormous amount of strength.« *Ines Papert*

I HAVE TWO whole days left at my disposal and I just simply have to try this route again. It is gigantic. Starting at the entrance, I follow a logical path up to the opening of the cave. After this, I want to climb over the roof of a cave from behind a seam. Then follow through the roof-edges. Then finish on a oute through a »Scottish« ice gully along the edges of a cliff. I am »armed« with a drill and hammer. We have to be quick. The clock is ticking.

»Jen Olsen climbs in »Ice Palace« WI5, the steep section in advance up to the cave, in order to patiently secure me during the ascent of the rock shelter.« *Ines Papert*

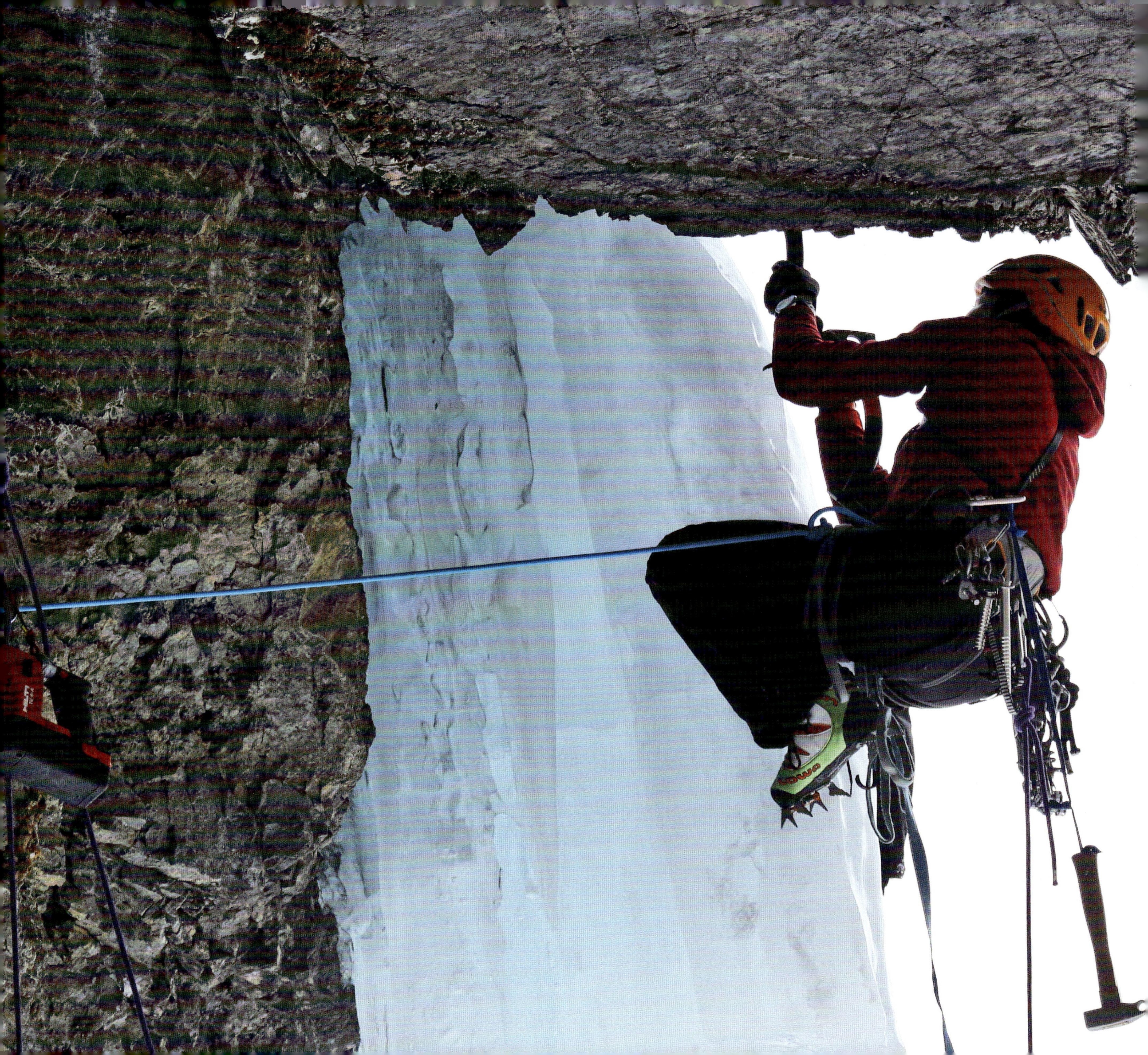

JEN PROVES how patient she is being my safety partner. The technical first ascent and drilling in on the route takes several hours and absorbs my power reserve completely. Tomorrow I want to succeed in getting through the route. At this point, I am physically and mentally finished.

Yet I know that my will and determination can move mountains. At 5 pm, I climb with Jon Walsh at twilight on our last legs. Nobody falls. Pink point. It is fantastic. I call this route »Into the Wild« and rate it with M12. To this day, it's still waiting for a repeat performance. On the following day at 8 am, the helicopter picks us up. At the eleventh hour, we are heading home with a huge achievement.

INTO THE WILD | M12/W15
HEIGHT OF THE FACE: 180 M
POSITION 51°51'35"N 116°55'50"W

NEPAL
KWANGDE SHAR
6.093 M

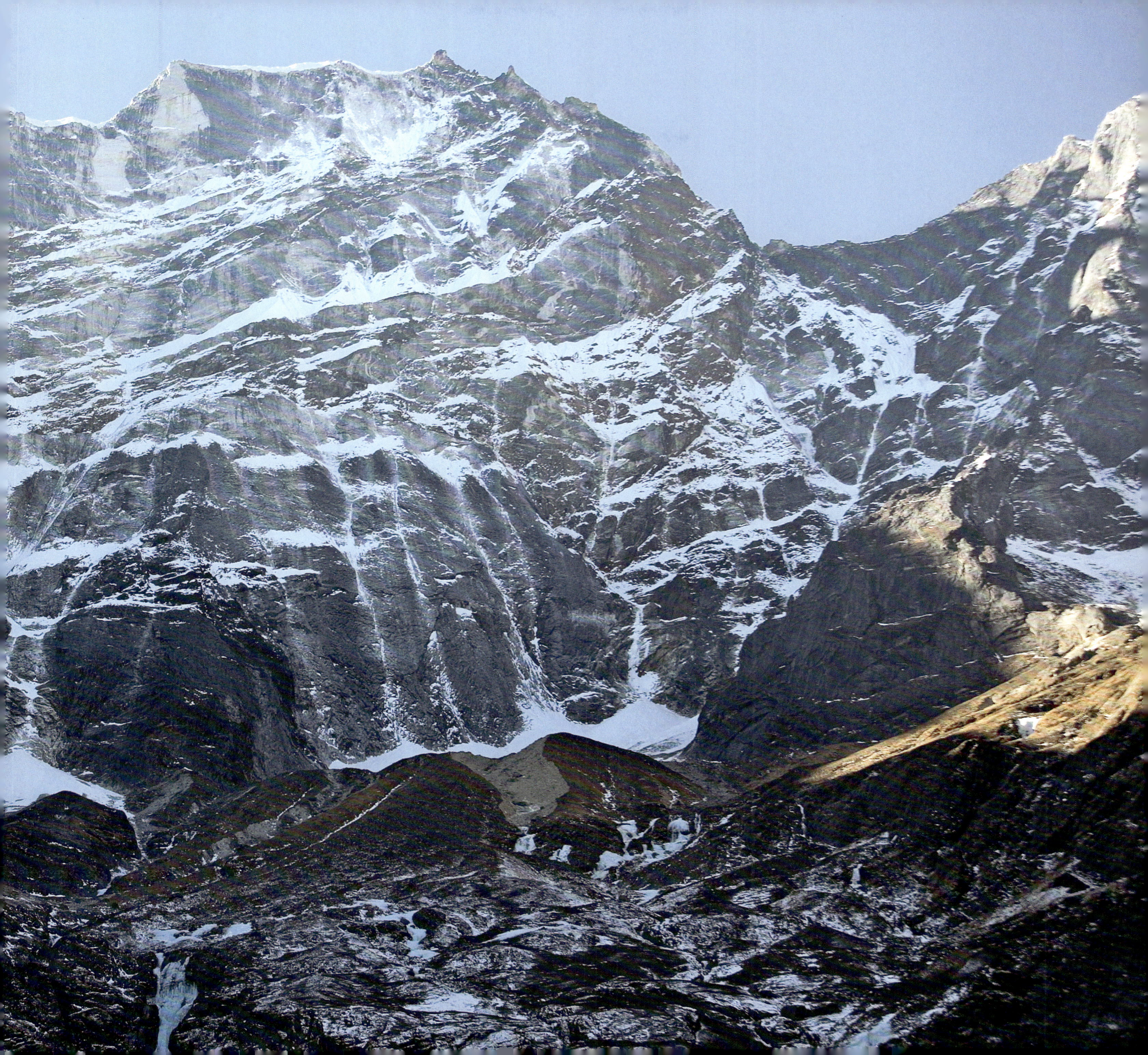

THIS IS THE FIRST Christmas I'm spending away from home. On the 24th December, we are celebrating in Namche Bazar. One last lukewarm shower, yak-cream-cheesecake and small presents for everyone. Jennifer Olsen, Audrey Gariepy and myself flew the route via Kathmandu to Lukla. According to the plan, the photographer Cory Richards will accompany us. Unlike the spring, when scores of mountain climbers leave from here in the direction of Mount Everest, the winter in Khumbu Valley is a lot quieter.

»On a three-day acclimatization tour across the Cho La Pass (5.420 metres) we are the only tourists around. After a Buddist Prayer Ceremony we finally set off for the mountain. Our Goal: Kwangde, 6.178 meters.
After a prayer ceremony, we finally head off in the direction of the mountain. Our destination: The 6.178 metres high Kwangde Lho.« *Ines Papert*

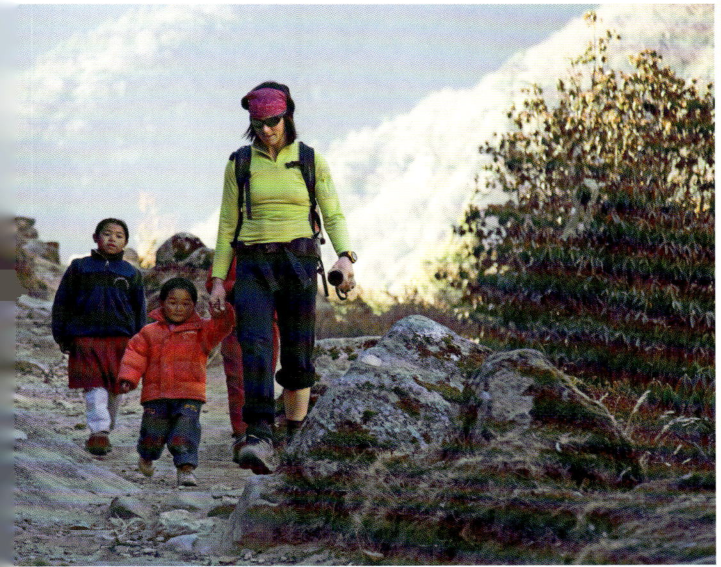

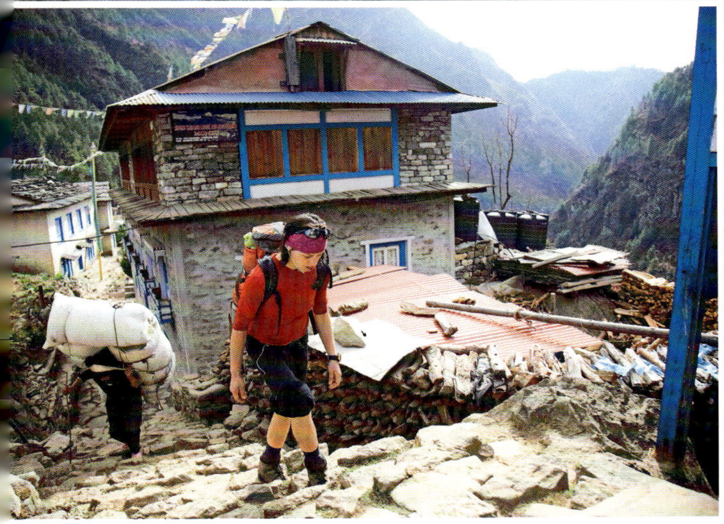

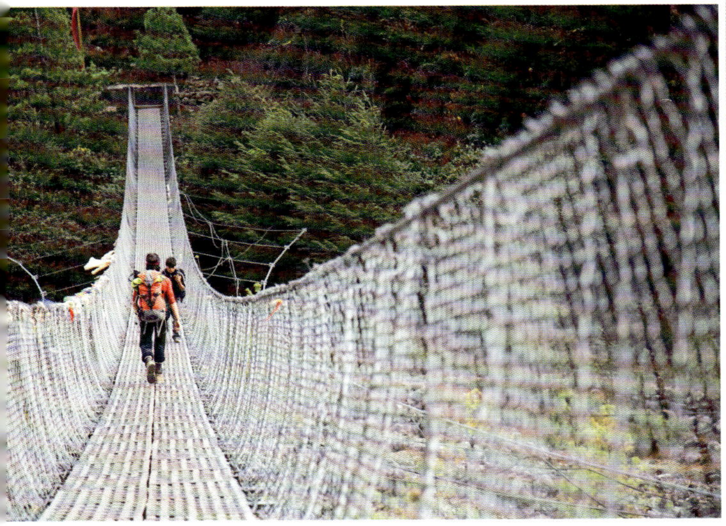

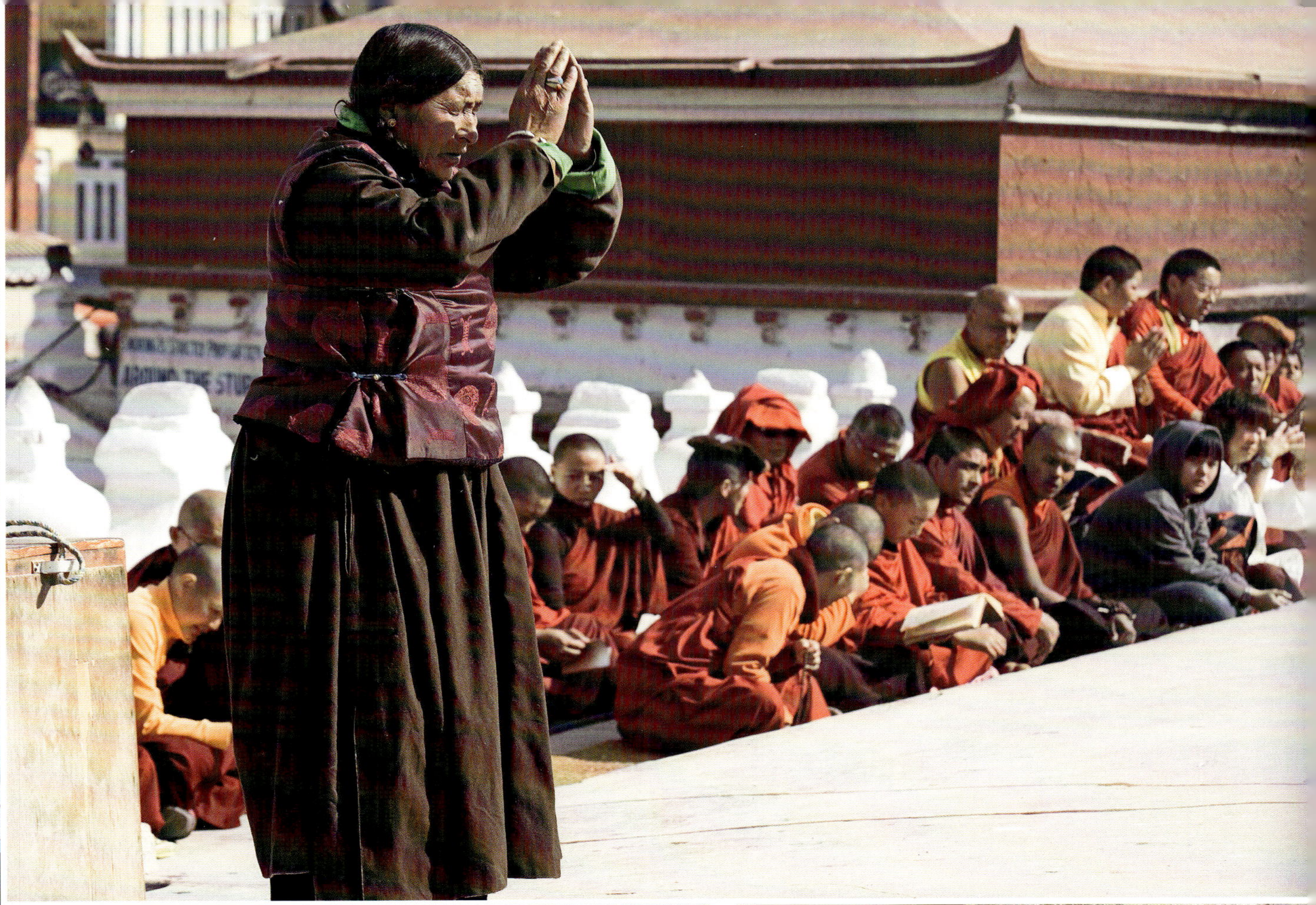

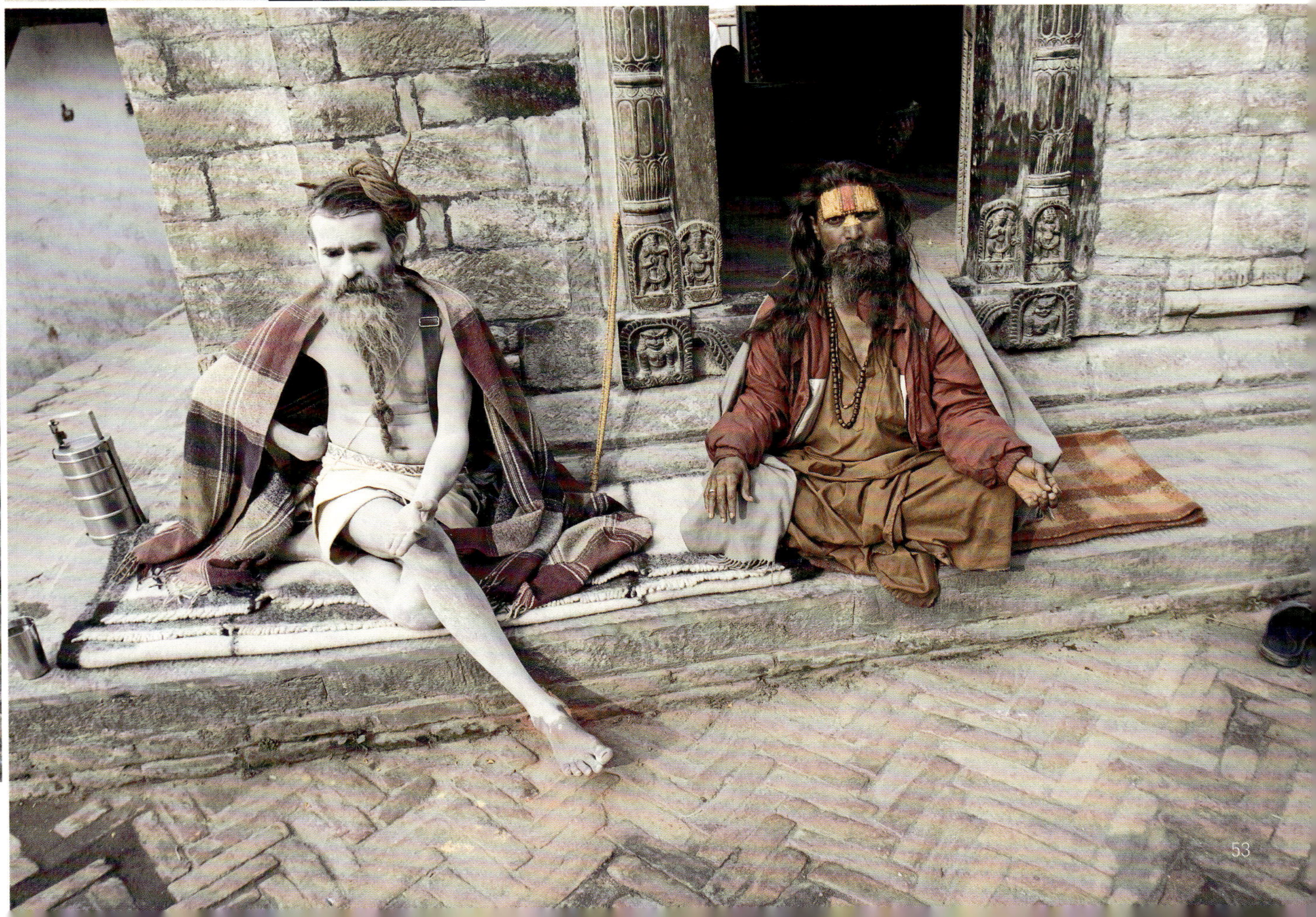

NEPAL

Kwangde Shar

Kathmandu Lukla

CHINA
BHUTAN
INDIA
BANGLADESH

WE ARE STANDING in front of the 1.400 metre high north face. How chilling! The conditions are less than ideal. Not enough ice and not enough snow. The route we had originally chosen for a first ascent can no longer be taken.

In search of an alternative, after a long period of twisting and turning, we finally agree to select a combination of existing routes in the right wall section. I admit, that the endless discussions are wearing me down. They are dampening my mood and joy. What keeps me going is the beauty and the vastness of the landscape. The dimensions here are simply tremendous. In comparison, we humans are tiny. Cory Richard's humour is priceless. It's not easy for him having to cope with three women. Audrey and I get on well with each other and we are always able to find a compromise. Jen makes her own decisions and by doing so, she unconsciously excludes herself. When she notices this, then she starts complaining. If it wasn't for Cory, we would probably never find a consensus.

We ladies decide to climb the north face. It is bitterly cold. Audrey complains about having numb fingers and toes, yet it doesn't seem to be anything to be worried about. Even after spending a very uncomfortable night in a bivvy at -20 degrees. The climbing is more difficult than we expected. We are about to withdraw from the north face and switch over to the southern side, in order to approach the summit from behind. Then it happens!

I climb ahead to belay both of my team colleagues and along the way I want to take something to drink. I take the thermos flask out of the backpack, retract the rope with the backstop and watch the open backpack glides away whooshing down the steep face. Satellite phone, walkie-talkie, headlamp, spare gloves and camera fall, in front of my eyes, out of the backpack and down the mountain! I am stunned. What do I do now? We can no longer communicate with base camp. However, we do have less weight to carry and we decide to keep going. We have to be extra cautious. We cannot afford to make any more mistakes. Around 2.30 pm, we manage to exit the north face. Roughly 400 metres in altitude lie on the southern side between us and the summit. We could possibly make it before sunset. However, we would have to rope down during the night. It's too dangerous. Also, we left our sleeping bags in the same place where we had slept last night. We turn back. It is extremely frustrating, yet we have no other choice.

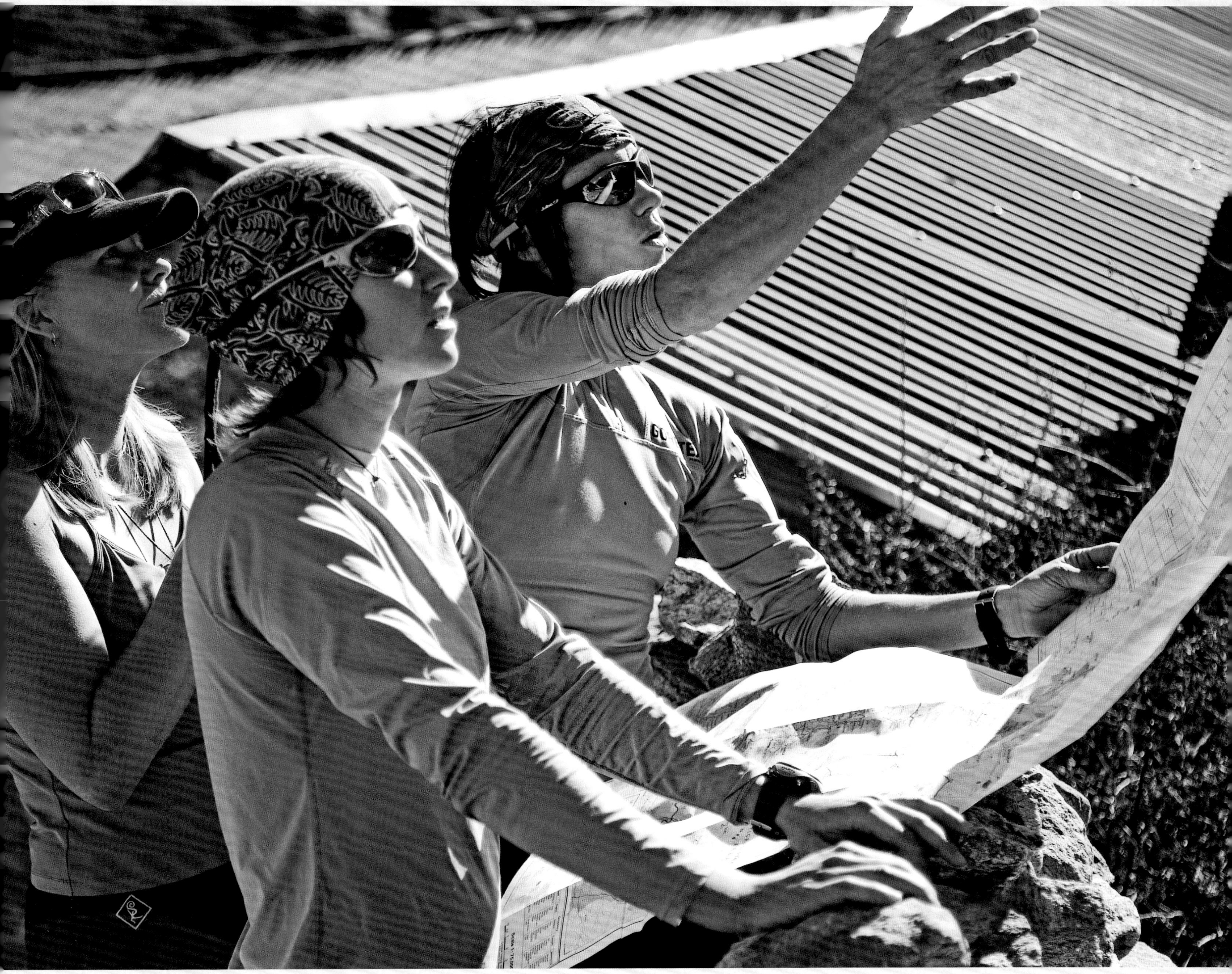

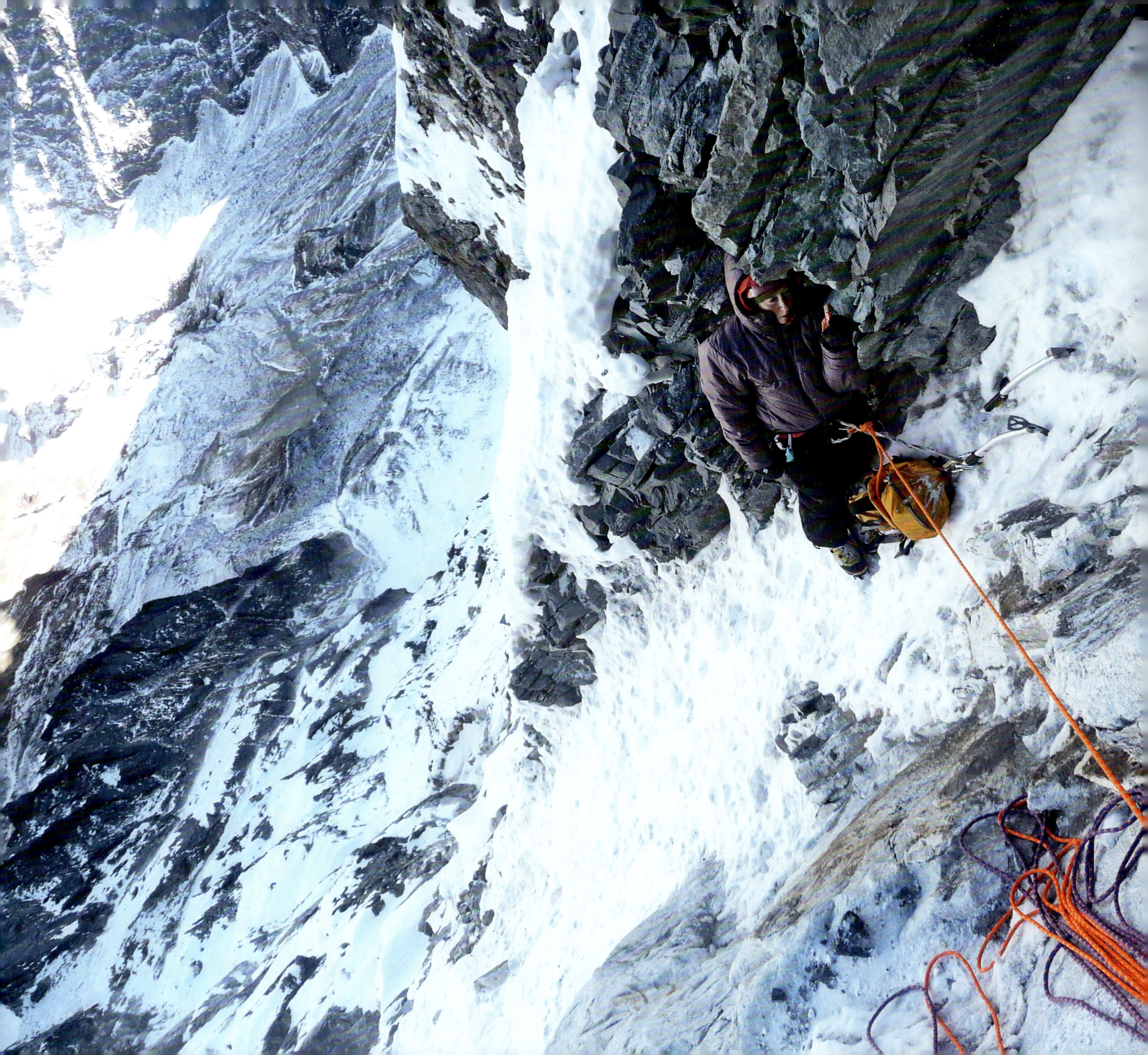

COMPLETELY EXHAUSTED, we rope down and reach the foot of the cliff. The low temperature is weighing on us. I am very sad, really frustrated. This is the second time in the Himalayas that I haven't been able to reach the peak. What another waste! Another failure! Audrey is suffering from nasty frostbites on her toes and has to go to hospital. It will be more than six months before she can walk again in proper shoes. Jen is no longer interested in making another attempt. She is also on her way home. Cory and I remain. We still have ten days. At least it's something.

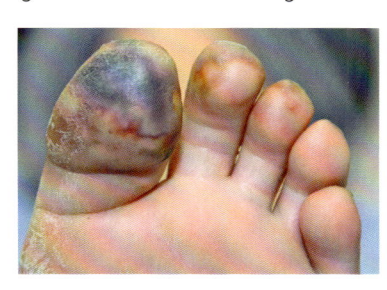

»Our backpack, including camera, fall down through the face 800 metres deep. Pictures? Not anymore.« *Ines Papert*

CORY IS NOT just a superb photographer. He is also a strong climber. It's his first time participating on a long expedition and he is extremely motivated. My proposal, to try climbing the north face of the Kwangde Shar, a neighbouring peak beside the Kwangde Lho, is music to his ears. Of course, he agrees. After spending a few days resting at our base camp, strategically planning and undergoing several packing activities, we're ready to start. Then, we're off. A new attempt! New opportunities? Our backpacks are awfully heavy. Due to the weight, our progress is very slow. We'll never make it at this pace! Cory is in great condition. I've more experience when it comes to climbing. Hence, we alter our strategy. Cory carries the extra weight, lowering the burden of my backpack, allowing me to climb in front. I am not sure whether men generally have a problem with letting women take charge and allowing to lead from the front. Cory is keeping his thoughts to himself. Our plan begins to bear fruit. Like clockwork. Very smoothly. Metre for metre and step by step, we start ascending.

»With Cory Richards forming a team of two, the access despite carrying heavy backpacks, is no problem. In a new constellation, we are extremely motivated to ascend the north face.« *Ines Papert*

»We are freezing in the bitter cold, longing for warm rays of sunshine. The last night spent in the bivvy was awful. In the background: Mount Everest.« *Ines Papert*

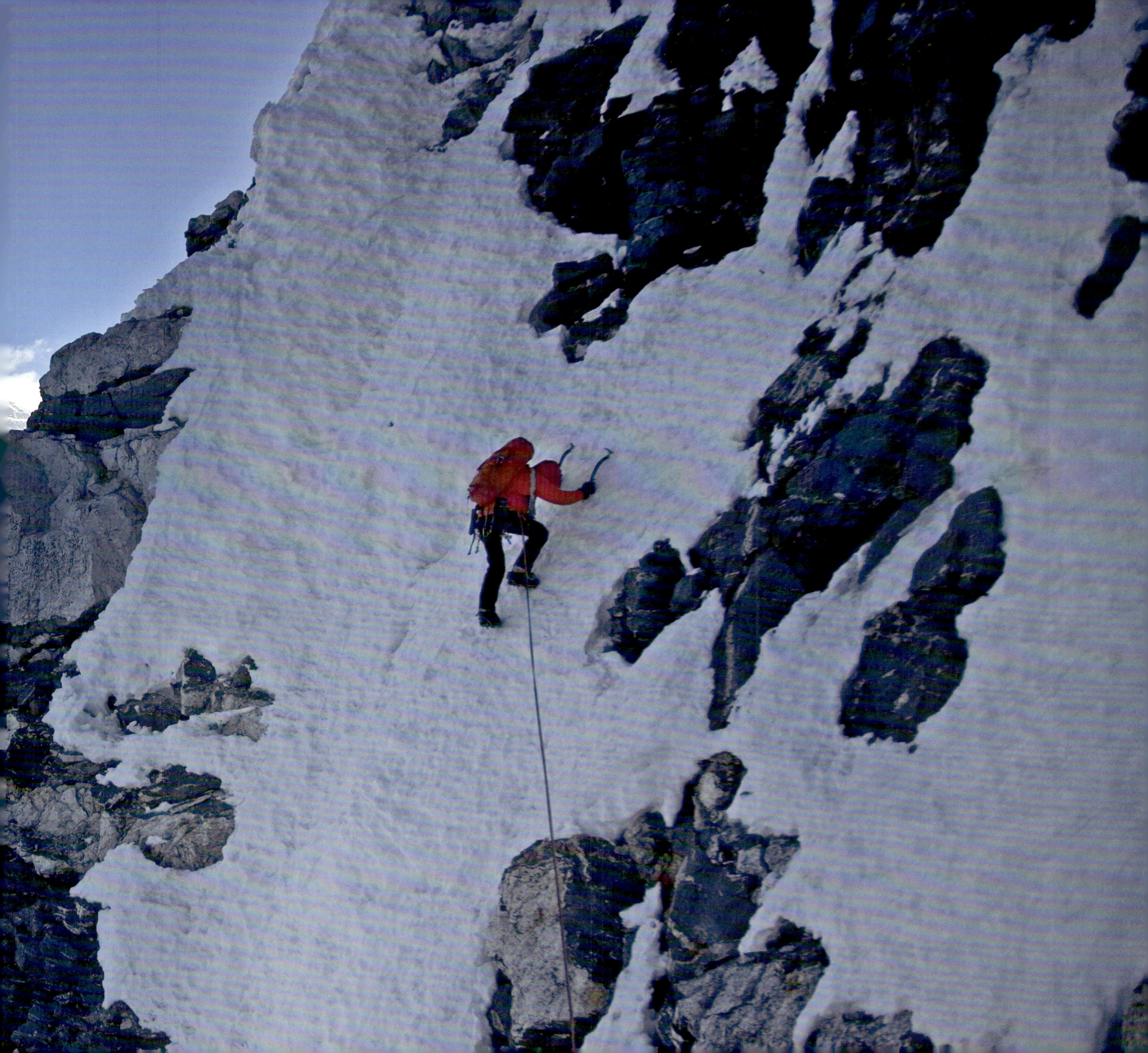

»On the last stretch towards the peak, the wall graciously leans back. This is our third day on the route to the peak. Our tears of joy quickly freeze to ice.« *Ines Papert*

THE WALL is very high and large. If I had set my sights on the peak at the beginning, all 1.400 metres of it, it would have knocked the breath out of me. Step by step. We think and plan from one bivvy to the next. No further. Stage for stage. Last night on the eastern edge was very hard. It was bitterly cold. Painfully uncomfortable. Simply awful. The first beams of sunlight work wonders for us. Balm for the soul. Hope for the tired body.

CONTRARY TO OUR assumption, some difficult terrain is waiting for us at the eastern ridge in the direction of the summit. Unpleasant plates and consistently difficult rocky slopes. We've spent three whole days plagued with this mountain and its face. We are definitely not stopping now. Around midday, we reach the highest point. The sunshine is deceptive. The wind, around the area of the summit, has grown into a full-blown jet stream, preventing every form of communication. Cory and I fall into each other's arms and begin to cry. In any case, words here are out of place.

We abseil on the other side of the mountain. A good day's walk and we'll reach our base camp. When we arrive, we enjoy the good food, and get lots of sleep. It's time to celebrate. Our very first summit in the Himalayas and the first ascent of our route. We're calling it »Cobra Norte«.

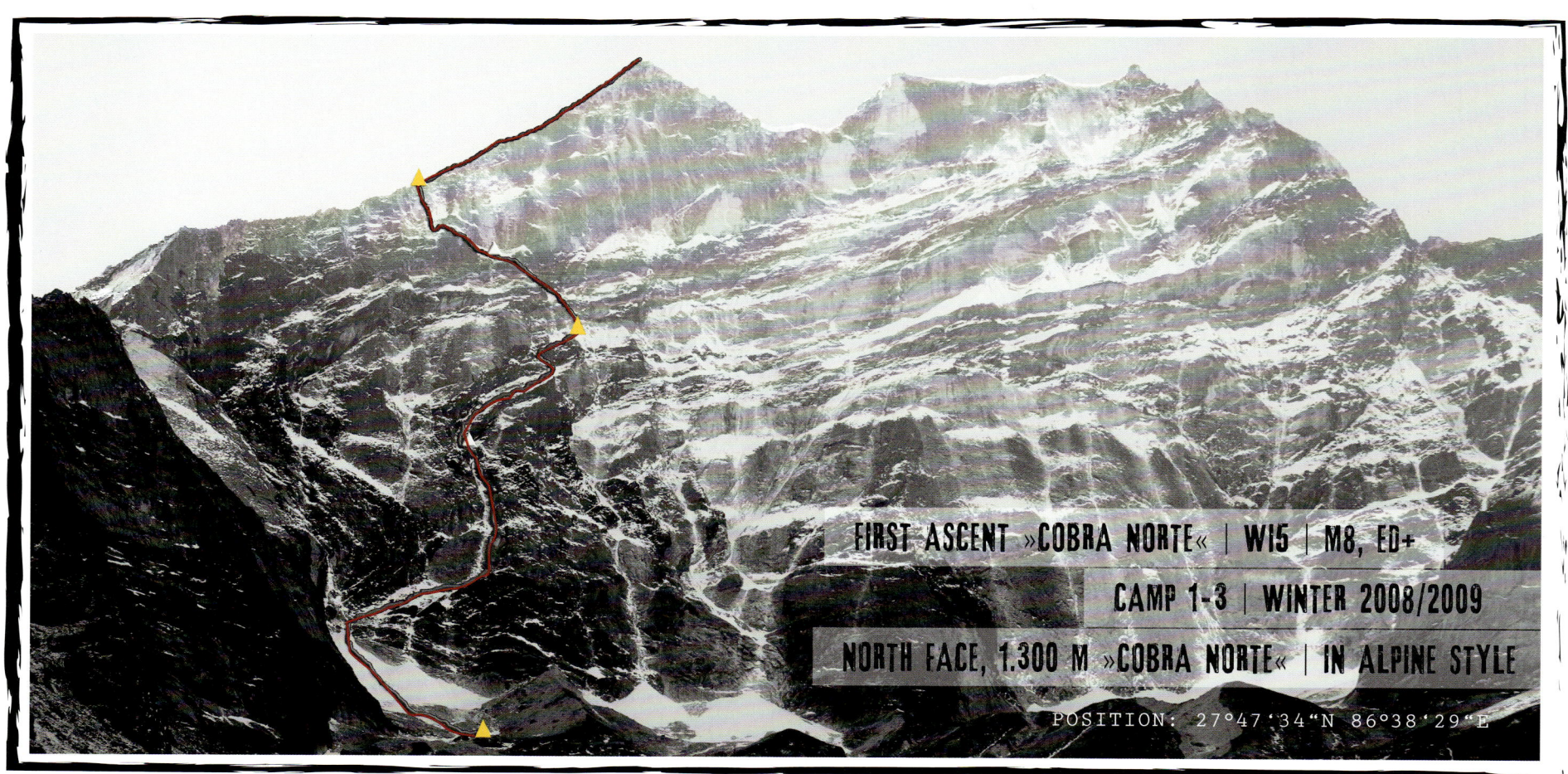

FIRST ASCENT »COBRA NORTE« | WI5 | M8, ED+
CAMP 1-3 | WINTER 2008/2009
NORTH FACE, 1.300 M »COBRA NORTE« | IN ALPINE STYLE
POSITION: 27°47'34"N 86°38'29"E

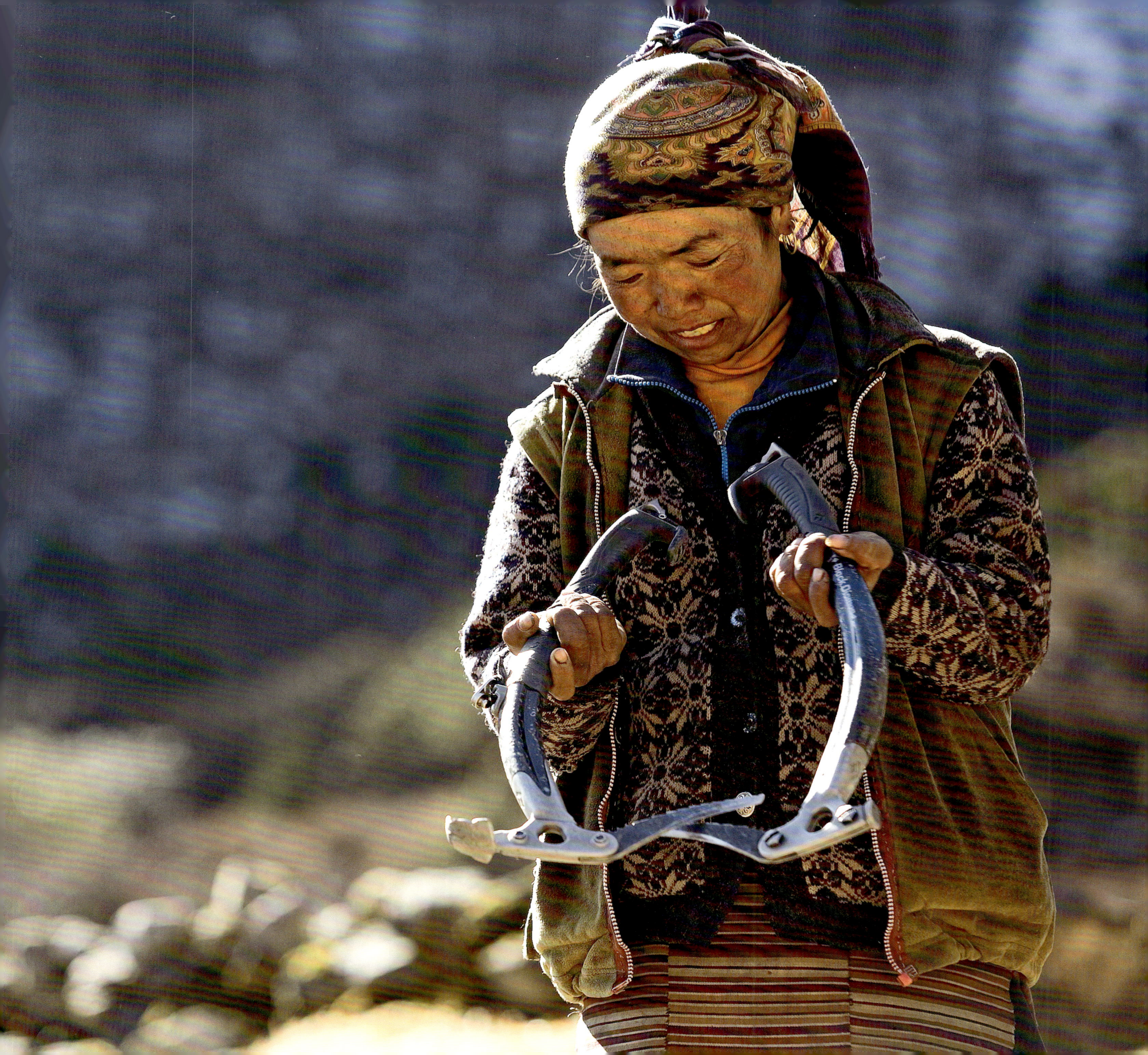

CANADA
CIRQUE OF THE UNCLIMBABLES

POSITION: 62°06'51.6''N 127°41'50.4''W

The Cirque of the Unclimbables lies in the Nahanni national park in the Canadian Northwest Terretories. In the Sixties, the area was discovered by a geological expedition. The walls or faces were named because the experts reckoned that they were »unclimbable«.

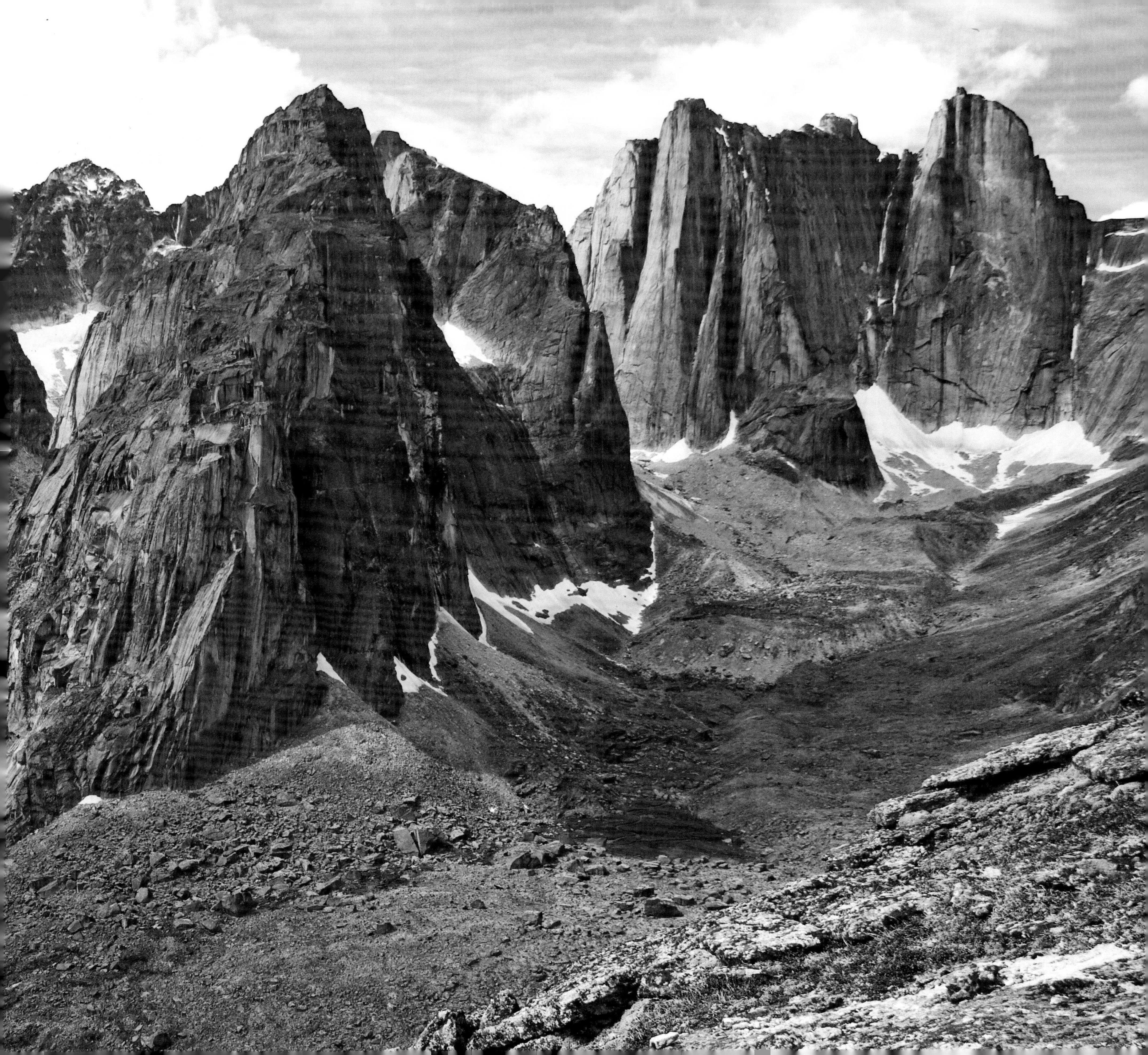

Landing with the floatplane on the Glacier Lake.

THERE ARE THREE ways to reach the Cirque of the Unclimbables. The exhausting and week-long journey with a kayak is not an option for Lisi and me. Taking a helicopter directly to the base camp at Fairy Meadows is also not an option. We opt for something »in-between«, still a troublesome solution, and we decide to fly with an aeroboat to Glacier Lake. A strenuous day-long march through jungle like forests and marshes separates us from our base camp, at the so-called Fairy Meadows. Loaded like donkeys, we set off. We have enough materials and food on our backs to last for three weeks.

MARC PICHÉ AND CHRIS ATKINSON, two photographers and good friends, who will report on the region, have travelled before us and they are awaiting our arrival. The Cirque of the Unclimbables is famous for its steep walls and notorious for its unpredictable weather. We have to be prepared for everything, including several days of adverse weather. For Lisi Steurer, our venture will be a real test in climbing on granite. First of all, we prepare by taping our hands, which will protect our skin from razor sharp cuts and wounds.

CANADA

Cirque of the Unclimbables

• Fort Nelson

• Calgary

Warm-up on the Penguin, the prominent rock pin in the Fairy Meadows.

IN THE FAIRY MEADOWS there are plenty of boulder blocks and opportunities to warm up for the larger climbs, such as one of the various sport climbing routes here called the »Penguin«. Most climbers head for the well-known Lotus Flower Tower. Within the Cirque it's swarming with steep cliffs, some of them not yet been developed. Lisi and I are well prepared and fully motivated. The camp stands. It's in good shape. The weather is fantastic. There is a tremendous prickling in the fingers as we take a look at the route at the East Huey Spire called »Riders on the Storm«. Nobody has ever tackled this by freeclimbing. That's a good enough reason to have a go.

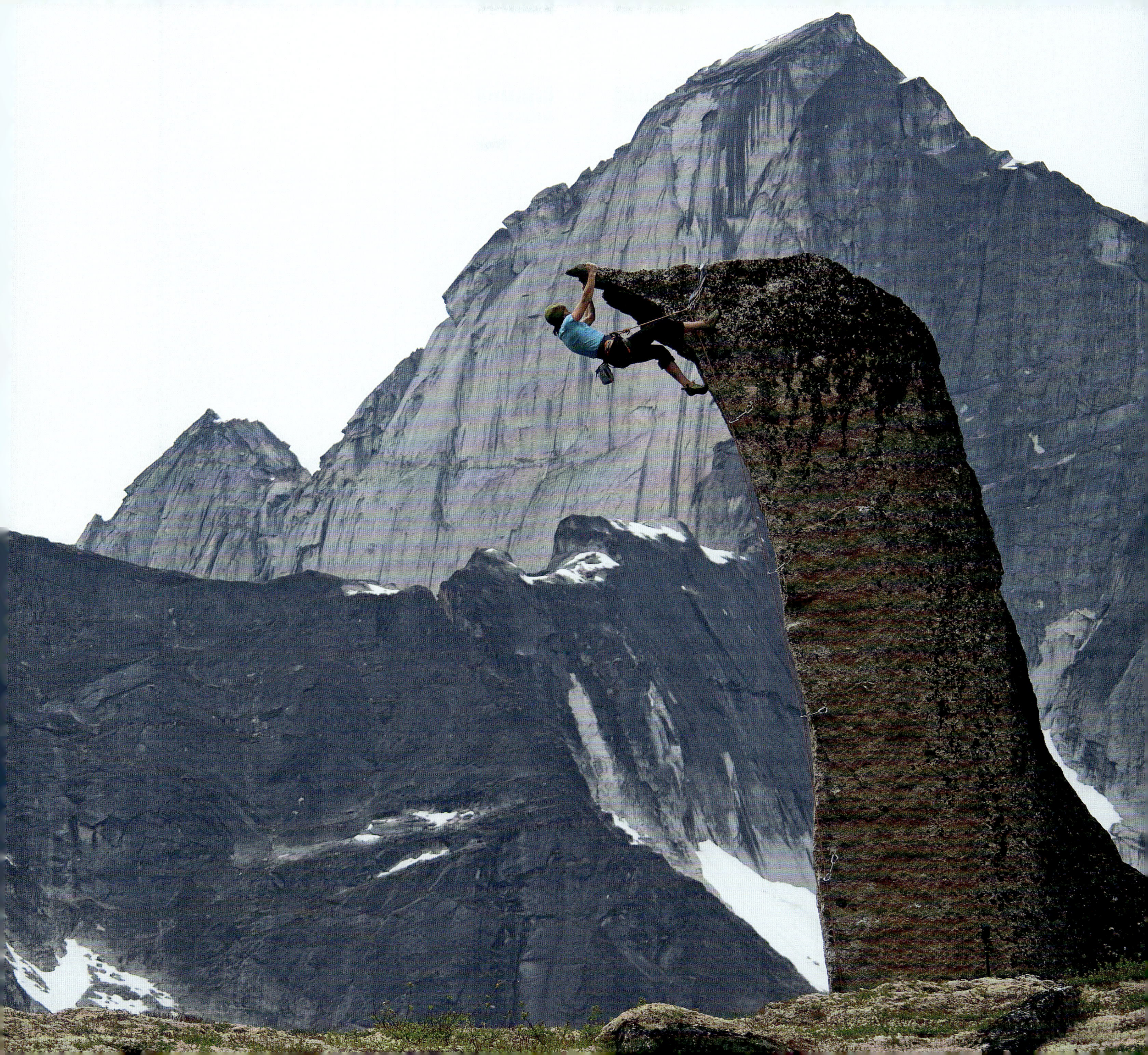

»We manage the first free climb on the 11-pitches-route on the East Huey Spire.«

RIDERS ON THE STORM | 5.12D (7C)

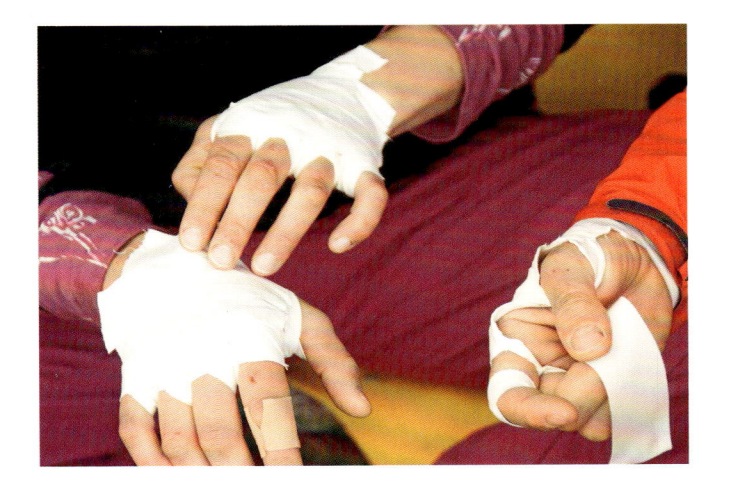

WE'VE SPENT two whole days dealing with the route going through the crack system. On several occasions, we've bouldered the cruces. On the third day, it starts to get serious. I succeed with the first ascent of »Riders on the Storm«. Of course, Lisi and I also want to climb the famous Lotus Flower Tower. Above its 800 metre high »South East Buttress«, we both climb up pretty fast to the peak in 9 ½ hours. We manage at the same time a fantastic onsight-climbing. The weather is too good to be true. A beautiful sunny day. It's been like this for the last two weeks. To be honest, we were expecting poor weather. This does have consequences. We've miscalculated the food portions.

We calculated that on days where we were expecting rain, we would be resting, and would only need between 500 and 800 calories per day. However, we are permanently in action and our calorie consumption per day is way too high. Our food is running out.

LOTUS FLOWER TOWER

SOUTHEAST BUTTRESS | 5.10C 800 M ONSIGHT IN 9.5 HOURS

»One has to be prepared for everything in the wilderness. We've been warned about black bears, although we haven't seen any around. Instead, on one occasion, I get the chance in the middle of nowhere to sit on an old pit latrine.« *Ines Paper*,

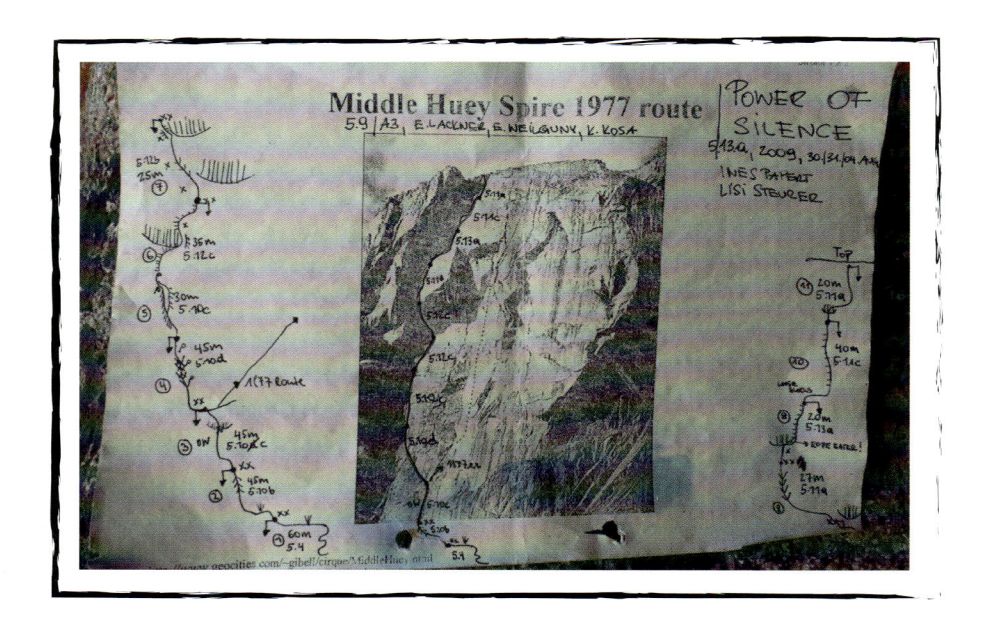

»The very finest intersection – and crack climbing. The tranquility in the wilderness gives us strength. Our route ›Power of Silence‹ is one of two routes through the largely overhung south face of the Middle Huey Spires. Its peak is solitary.« *Ines Papert*

THE WEATHER IS too good for taking breaks. Furthermore, at this latitude in the summertime, we can expect 20 hours of daylight. At the Middle Huey Spire in 1977, an Austrian expedition ventured through the south face. Since then, nobody else has tackled it. Lisi and I want to try it. The route that the Austrians took goes through fragile rocks. A more logical yet also difficult route, we follow an intersection system on the left wall section. Then we climb over huge hanging walls. Whenever possible, we only use mobile safety clips. After spending three days of preparation, we both reach the peak of the Middle Huey Spire. This is Lisi's first major ascent. An exciting question remains, if we can carry out a successful passage. A day's rest and two further days of practise, where we burst through the path, I succeed getting through the route. After spending several days here on our own, we baptize this route »Power of Silence«.

POWER OF SILENCE | 5.13- (7C+)

GEAR: BOLTED BELAYS AND FIVE ADDITIONAL BOLTS IN THE ROUTE MOST OF IT CLEAN, CAMELOTS AND NUTS.
FIRST ASCENT AND FREE CLIMB | HEIGHT OF FACE: 500 M

SCOTLAND ROADTRIP

»My experience in Scotland has a lasting effect on my attitude to climbing in clean style.« *Ines Papert*

WINTER CLIMBING in Scotland is fascinatingly thankless. You have to invest in long approaches before you even get to touch the cliff. The weather is so changeable and moody, that you have to take everything into consideration. Often, only a few hours lie between bright sunshine and snow storms.

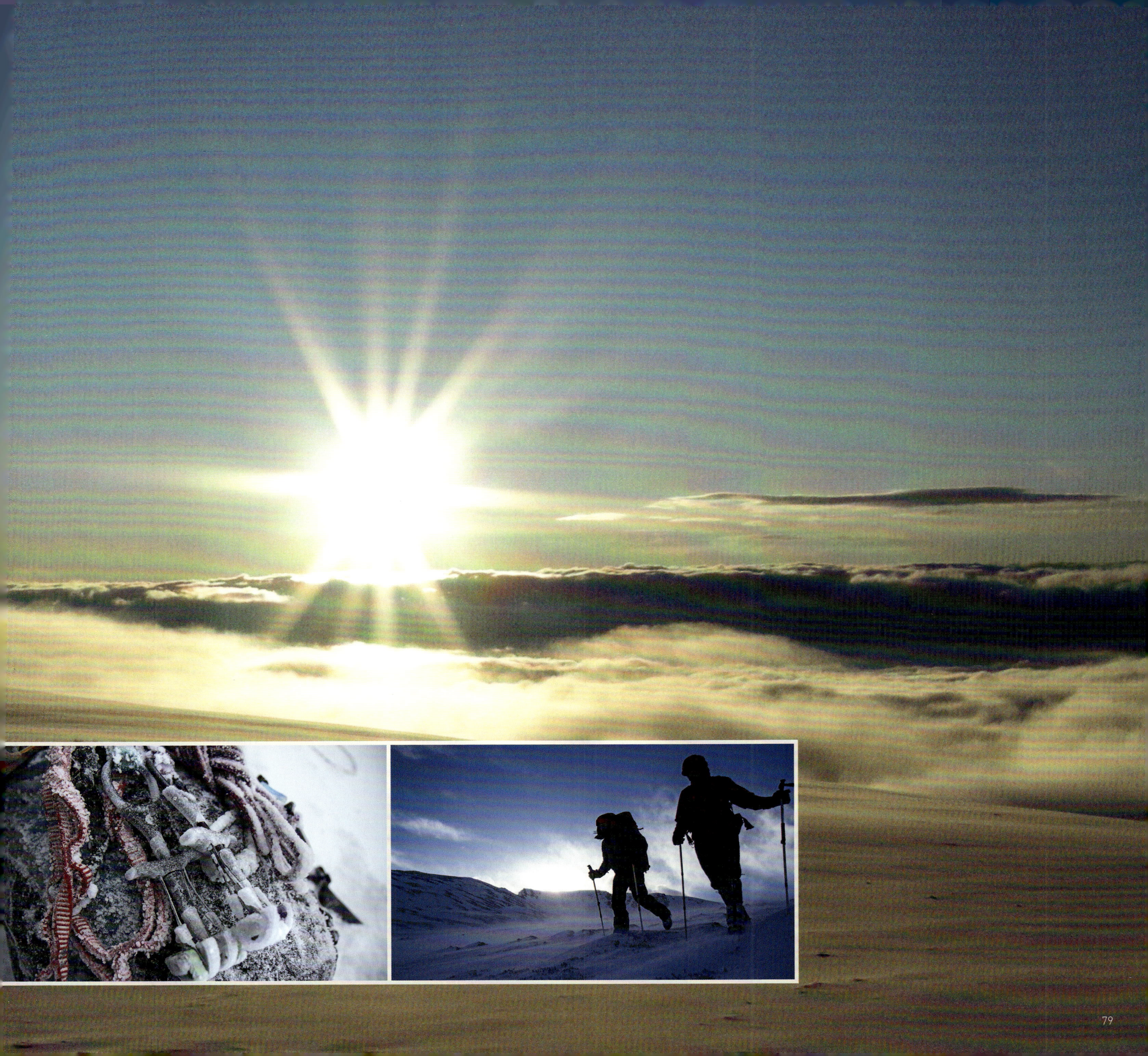

»On the peak of Ben Nevis, we unexpectedly meet a friendly local man, Dave MacLeod, and agree to meet up together the next day, to complete a first ascent.« *Ines Papert*

Charly Fritzer climbs »The Demon Direct« IX, 9 onsight | Cairngorms, Coire an Lochain.

DOING WITHOUT BOLTS is the law in Scotland. The climbing here is traditional and that means solely with mobile safety devices. I have gained a lot of respect, due to hearing dramatic stories about awful falls and accidents. In order to see it for myself, I travel to Scotland in the wintertime. For the record: Without the support of the local climbers, who gave me a lot of information and hints, I wouldn't have been able to climb more than a few winter classics. Because of this support, my road trip through Scotland developed into a unique adventure and a memorable experience. It would have a lasting effect on my attitude towards bolt-free, traditional climbing. Ian Parnell, a very strong Scottish climber and experienced Himalaya-alpinist, supported me and introduced me to several local climbers.

»You are so lucky, Scotland's winter climbs are in perfect conditions.« *Ian Parnell*

SCOTLAND

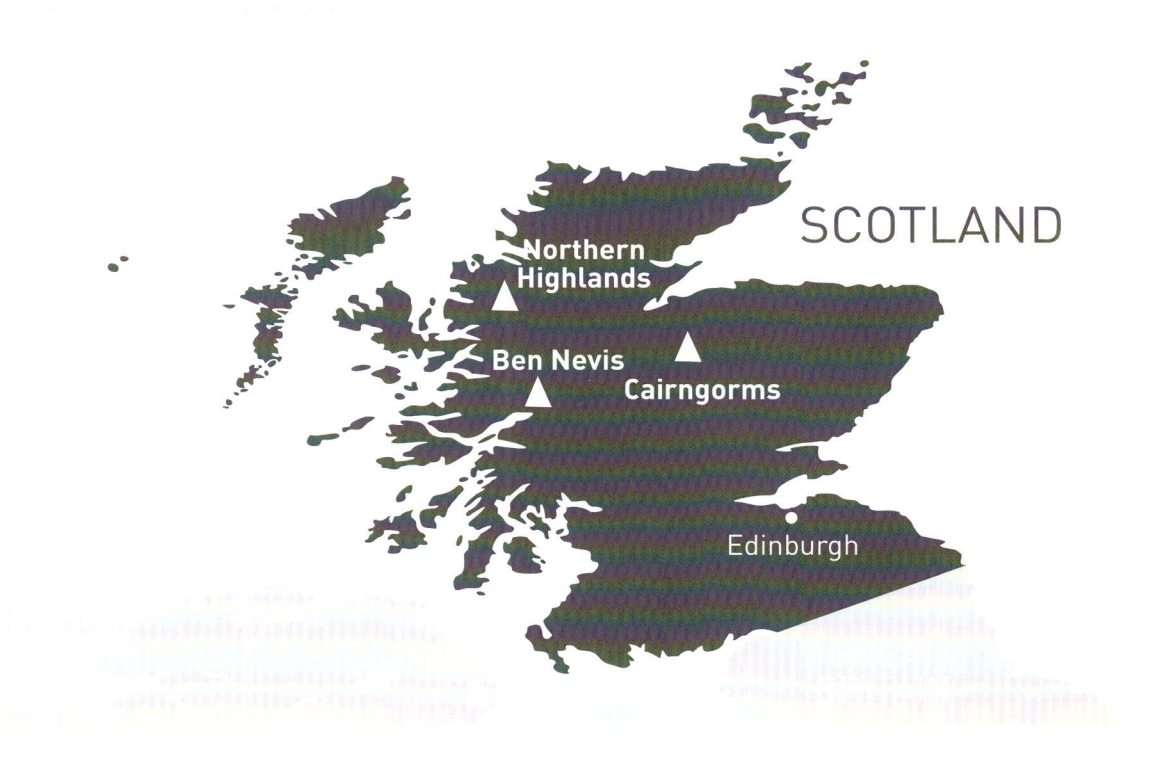

SIMON YEARSLEY lends me his »Big Tree Campervan«. I climb with various partners in different regions: Ben Nevis, in the northern highlands and in the Cairngorms. The van: It's my mobile home, with many visitors coming and going.

I like the Scots and their mentality. Warmhearted people, open and very helpful. They would give you their last shirt, if they had to. The climbers are very proud and are delighted to hear when you are enthusiastic about their country. I spend very exciting days with Audrey Gariepy, Charly Fritzer, Ian Parnell, Dave MacLeod, Greg Boswell, Pete MacPherson and Michael Tweedley, where we repeat first ascents and establish new routes. Hans Hornberger accompanies us with his camera. It's a real challenge under such uncomfortable conditions to take such good pictures.

BLOOD, SWEAT AND FROZEN TEARS VIII (8) ON BEN EIGHE IN THE NORTHERN HIGHLANDS.

THE STRONG ETHICS of the Scots impress me. As mentioned, you needn't start to think about bolts. One has to be mentally prepared, to solely depend on mobile safety devices. Ian is like a mentor to me. In difficult rock passages covered in white frost and snow, you need to have the confidence to trust the mobile safety devices, which can slip easily. By the way: If a face is black in winter, which is not covered in »Rime« or white frost, then it is not worth climbing at all. It is useless and isn't recognized as a winter ascent. That's the way the Scots are.

Cosy in the campervan. With Hans Hornberger, Audrey Gariepy and Mat Audibert.

HAPPY TYROLEANS
X/10 ONSIGHT | CAIRNGORMS

Charly Fritzer manages the first free repeat.

>A ripening combination of high humidity, wind and temperatures around freezing point occurs. >Rime< covers the cliff with a plastic-like structure which – in contrast to ice – gives little or no stability. My ice tools have to fit well into the cracks if I want to climb safely. I cannot imagine a better preparation for the technically more demanding high mountains.< *Klaus Kranebitter*

TO THOSE WHO WAIT
IX/9 | BEN NEVIS

»Local Ian Panell does a good job being my mentor.« *Ines Papert*

FIRST I HAVE to win my »Scottish Wings«. As a climber, you can't expect any favours from Scottish winters. I sometimes find it difficult to leave the warm van at night to march off at sea level. It takes hours until we finally get to the foot of the wall. We've usually covered over 1.000 metres in altitude. Sometimes in the snow storm, sometimes in the drizzle, very seldom do we get any sun. This is what is so fascinating about Scotland. It's part of the game. If you are waiting for the weather to improve, then you will lose. Here you get the chance to prove to yourself, how strong your will really is. In order to take a shower, we occasionally spend a night in a youth hostel. Apart from this, we also get to dry our very wet ropes and clothes. Even if our campervan is cosy, the heating inside it cannot really compete with Scottish winters.

MY FIRST ASCENTS:
LITTLE NIPPER | VI | 8 | NORTHERN HIGHLANDS | BEN EIGHE 2010 WITH IAN PARNELL
TRIPLE X | VIII | 8 | BEN NEVIS 2011 WITH DAVE MACLEOD/CHRALY FRITZER
BAVARINTHIA | IX | 9 | CAIRNGORMS | COIRE AN LOCHAIN 2011 WITH CHARLY FRITZER

FRIENDS & COMPANIONS

DEPARTURE AND HOMECOMING –
I AM LONGING FOR BOTH

Once or twice a year, I hit the road – off on a new adventure. Regardless of how stressful the planning and preparation for an expedition is – especially close to the beginning – the idea of leaving on a journey into the unknown, inspires me. When the aim and the team are set, it's only then that I find training easier to do. Then I usually spend hours in my office researching and organizing the new tour.

Before heading off, I always throw a little party for my family and closest friends at home in Bayerisch Gmain. This get together is a ritual for me. Now I admit, that I am sad when it is time to say goodbye. However, I get excited about the possibility of setting off on a new journey. I am fully aware that I lead a very privileged life and I am most grateful. I have a close knit circle around me that allow me to pursue my way of life. Manu's father, my former partner, along with the two grandmothers, look after our son when I am on an expedition. Knowing Manu is in the best hands allows me to concentrate on and look forward to my expeditions. When I am away for longer periods of time, I begin to miss not being at home. When I spend a lot of time at home, I look forward to the next expedition. Strange, isn't it? How both influence one another. Departing and arriving home. I drift through life between the two – and yes, I am immensely satisfied.

People often ask me, what criteria I select when choosing my expedition and rock-climbing teams. The answer is simple and frank. I am looking for people that I value and can rely on.

It's not just having a passion for the same activity. It's not just having the same goals (at least for a fixed period of time). This is too simple. It's also not just having an umbilical cord tied to one another and being able to totally rely on each another. That's logical. The people I travel with on exhibitions have to be very close to me. So close, that we can share a bivvy together, and so close that we can spend endless days in a tent together, peacefully, under bad weather conditions on the other side of the world. The most important criterion for me is the amount of fun we can have. The ideal partner is not necessarily the one with the best ability to climb. We have to suit one another on a personal level and also under pressurising and unpleasant circumstances. It is easy to be in a pessimistic mood when things are going wrong. It is more difficult to remain quiet and positive, holding on to one's sense of humour and restraining oneself. These are the qualities in a person that I highly value. Yes, I am familiar to tears, heated disputes and fairly serious dramas on exhibitions. In such extreme situations, you not only take a look at yourself, you also take a look at the other team members' souls. Sometimes, that can be something quite difficult for all of those involved.

ANDES KANG HUA I have wonderful memories of my time with Ines during the Harbin Ice Festival. Being able to climb with a world-class athlete like her was a terrific experience. I learnt a lot from Ines and hope that we will soon stand together on a real summit in my home country of China.

ANITA KOLAR When Ines and I tested the mini skis at the Grossglockner for the ascent to and descent from the Arwa Tower, she did a few elegant swings and then patiently waited for me while I was hardly able to stand upright on my skis on the melt-freeze crust. With her solution-oriented manner, Ines organised a round sled for me at the Arwa Tower with which I sled down the 1.000 metres in height from the ABC to the base camp as swift as lightning.

»I enjoy sharing an expedition with women just as much as men. Mixed teams also operate very well. I don't have any preference. What differentiates me from the other mountaineers is that I like to regularly switch climbing partners. There are of course several people with whom I've been on many tours with, due to the excellent teamwork together.«

Ines Papert

AUDREY GARIEPY Ines is a fantastic climbing partner, always chirpy and game for virtually anything. She loves what she does and that comes across at the other end of the rope. The fact that she has remained so humble despite her successes underpins the great person Ines is. To me, she is a source of inspiration.

CAROLINE GEORGE I met Ines during her first World Cup. Even though she was climbing in plastic shoes and with outdated ice-climbing equipment, she came second right away. We immediately realised that she would soon make it to the very top with state-of-the-art equipment. And that's precisely what happened. Once I had decided to have a baby, I oriented myself towards Ines. She is a role model for many women. You can satisfy your passion and still (or, because of that?) be a good mother.

CHRIS ATKINSON When John Irvine from Arc'teryx booked me for a film shoot with Ines and Harri Berger in the Grand Wall of Squamish, I was impressed by Ines' talent and drive after the first day. Over time, however, I realised that her enthusiasm extends far beyond climbing. Her constant demand for good coffee and ice-cream, which is easily met in Chamonix, Squamish and even Kathmandu, is remarkable. You should have seen Ines' face once she finally realised, in the solitude of the Cirque of the Unclimbables, that there was no hope whatsoever of getting either cappuccino or ice-cream.

EMANUELLE CIULLO I met Ines when she made a presentation in the Grödner valley. I was astonished how motivated and enthused she related her climbing adventures. In Norway, I was able to see for myself what is was like to be out and about with her. All I can say is: she is well capable of asserting herself as the only woman among five men! We had a lot of fun with Ines. She is uncomplicated and really funny.

GREG BOSWELL When I met Ines on the parking lot of the Cairngorm ski centre a few years ago during a snow storm, I didn't have any idea how much this meeting would inspire me. She is a real bundle of energy and seems to enjoy climbing, even in the worst kind of weather. Meeting Ines has inspired me to go to my limits occasionally.

HANS HORNBERGER Being out and about with Ines as a photographer is a physical and mental challenge. Generally, you can expect long ascents to difficult, exposed routes. Thanks to her motivation and energy, however, the hard work really is great fun. When I view the pictures in the evening I always think: »What a day!«

CORY RICHARDS Honestly, my life would not be the same had I not met Ines. She was like a tidal wave of energy that pushed me ahead in my development as a climber and as a person. Without her I would never have had the opportunity of climbing in Asia and the Himalaya for the first time. If I had attempted to climb the Kwangde with anyone else I would have failed. Ines was the driving force during the ascent. Luckily I was able to take part and watch her talents unfold. Ines' drive is catching, her passion boundless. She pursues her goals persistently and single-mindedly. Sometimes she loses sight of the fact that she needs to switch back a gear or even give up. But that's Ines. It's all part and parcel.

DAVE MACLEOD I had the pleasure of opening up a new route on Ben Nevis with Ines and Charly in winter. Watching Ines climb in the difficult terrain, in which it is hard to belay someone, is impressive. Every move looks relaxed, controlled and »easy«. But only for as long as you don't climb yourself. Ines is a brilliant ice climber.

FRANZ WALTER No unusual experience: meeting place – airport. An exhausted Ines arrives. Up to a few hours ago we only had a confirmation of our reservation, no tickets. A fact that Ines only noticed the day before. Once again she succeeded in sorting things out just before we were due to depart. Nietzsche once quite aptly wrote: »You must have chaos within you to give birth to a dancing star.« To me, Ines is an incorruptible, curious person, an ambitious, professional athlete of a lifetime and, above all, a reliable and honest friend.

HARI BERGER | **Kirsten Buchmann on behalf of Hari Berger:** Hari was often out and about with Ines and really enjoyed it. To him, it was her uncomplicated manner that was instrumental. Also, Hari appreciated good food and Ines is happy to tuck in. Had Hari lived longer he would most likely have stood in his very own »Soul Kitchen« one day. That was his dream. And Ines, I am sure, would have been one of his regulars.

IAN PARNELL I wonder what Ines thought the first time she travelled to Scotland in the winter. Most climbers are frustrated: lots of rain, no bolts, long ascents, no M grades ... However, Ines immediately felt comfortable here and impressively proved how much fun you can have with two ice picks despite all odds. »All« you have to do is be prepared to give your all.

JOHANNA STÖCKL As a journalist who writes regular reports on Ines I am a rare species in this distinguished circle. So far, I have neither hung off a rock face with Ines nor did I ever spend a night with her in a tent. I have, however, experienced exciting days with Ines in the Chinese megacity Harbin. A memorable moment? When we were invited for dinner at Chen's parents and Ines – after downing a few shorts – gave a fiery speech that not only moved me to tears.

»However, new constellations basically don't have any burdens. They are fresh, exciting, inspiring, lively and an enrichment. Compared with other climbers, I haven't had much luck with the magic number »3«. Others prefer to be in teams of three. In my opinion, when groups of three are climbing together, there is always a danger, that one member inadvertently gets left out – at least that is the person feels, for part of the tour. That's why I prefer to be out and about with somewhat larger teams.« *Ines Papert*

DENNIS BURDET I have known Ines since Interlaken, before we travelled to India together. In Delhi we happily checked out Indian delicacies – after a few days all in our group, bar Ines, were ill. Anyone who has seen her shoulders knows how strong this woman is. | **STEPHAN SIEGRIST** Ines is in no way inferior to us men. She is one of the most awesome all-round mountaineers I know. Her fighting spirit and sheer willpower impressed me from the word »go«. But what impresses me even more is that Ines has remained so humble despite her success and is a very loving and caring mother to her son Manu. | **THOMAS SENF** Being out and about with Ines is fantastic. As if I was travelling with my big sister. The fact that Ines also has a life outside climbing and mountains, although she makes her living from it, really impresses me. Maybe more so than her outstanding climbing skills.

JEN OLSEN I have experienced quite a few bizarre situations with Ines, for example in the Bugaboos, where a horrific storm took us by surprise. On our Nepal expedition we had lost a backpack in the north face of the Kwangde Lho, which did not stop Ines wanting to continue on to the summit – even though we were late and did not have any safety reserves due to the loss. In this situation, I criticised the irrepressible will I normally admire in her, alongside her physical strength. The fact that Ines manages to accommodate climbing and being a mother commands my respect.

JON WALSH Luckily I have had lots of great experiences with Ines on gorgeous expeditions. Her enthusiasm for climbing is catching. Be it on a rock face or on ice, in difficult terrain in the mountains or even during training in a hall: to Ines it is important that it is fun. That is why I am looking forward to further adventures with her.

JOSHUA LAVIGNE Ever since our expedition to Baffin Island I know from personal experience why Ines is considered one of the best mountaineers in the world. She is exceptionally fit, very experienced with regard to mountaineering issues and stays calm and collected even in difficult situations. A phrase I frequently hear from her is: »I will try.« I believe that this casual sentence contains the secret of expedition mountaineering. As soon as our expectations vanish into thin air and only willpower and ambition remain, success can happen.

KURT ASTNER I still remember how Ines held little Manu on her arm in the isolation zone in Pitz valley. Back then, I thought that the woman knew precisely what she wanted. A few years later she was the world ice climbing champion. I am always happy when Ines contacts me, be it for a sport climb or to climb a pinnacle route. Like myself, she is somewhat chaotic and tends to do many things at the same time. But she's always in a good mood. In an era where records and superlatives is all that counts, I value the fact that Ines is a person with whom one can even enjoy the time after the climb.

LISI STEURER As women, the approach we take to climbing and possibly also to life unites us. We are neither better nor worse, stronger or weaker than our male colleagues. The battle between the sexes in mountaineering – and outside it as well – should finally end. Climbing makes me happy and Ines also primarily climbs because she enjoys it. And, while we're at it: famous female ›firsts‹ or similar aren't our cup of tea – whatsoever.

LIV SANSOZ Many years ago I met Ines during the world ice climbing championship. Not only is she a terrific athlete, she is also a wonderful person and a loyal, generous friend. Climbing means a lot to her but is not the be all and end all. That is what I really value in Ines. I am looking forward to many more adventures with her!

MARC PICHÉ If you are planning to spend many weeks in the wild with people you never saw before in your life that can go horribly wrong. That is why I was nervous waiting with Chris Atkinson in the Cirque of Unclimbables for Ines and Lisi. Armed with a hand saw I had tried to render the completely overgrown path from Glacier Lake to the camp more easily accessible. When the girls eventually turned up, loaded down like mules, enveloped in a cloud of insects, with grazed legs and arms, bathed in sweat but beaming radiantly, I knew we would have a great time.

RUDI HAUSER My tours and experiences with Ines are always characterised by mutual respect and athletic ambition. Discipline and perseverance are some of Ines' greatest skills when climbing. I don't want to comment on Ines private life as it wouldn't be private anymore if I did.

SEBASTIAN TISCHLER Film shoots with Ines are fun. Ines always ensures that, as a camera operator, I arrive safely at a good location. Quite a feat, considering my limited mountaineering skills. Thanks Ines for letting me accompany your activities occasionally!

LUKAS SEIWALD I haven't known Ines for all that long and so I can't really comment. What I can say is that Ines is a great person to be around!

MONI KALLSPERGER I really enjoy being out and about with Ines as she does not have a blinkered approach to mountaineering and is open to other things in life. What genuinely touched me were the many tears of joy that Ines shed when we were back at the rock face for the very first time after her horrific accident in the Dolomites.

»I want to dedicate one of the chapters in this book to those who have accompanied me on my rock-climbing tours and expeditions. None of the adventures mentioned here in this book would have been possible without them. I wish to convey my gratitude to all of those who have escorted me on my travels. I thank you for the very valuable experiences and time we have shared, including the ups and downs, conquering the mountains together.« *Ines Papert*

SIMON YEARSLEY My first encounter with Ines was typical. At night, on a dark parking lot in Scotland she extended her hand and said: »Hi Simon, come on, let's go climbing!« I love her enthusiasm for climbing. What do I have great respect for? The fact that she is one of the real hard core winter climbers in Scotland. Is there anything negative I can say about Ines? Yes! She is not used to drinking good Scotch whisky.

WOLFGANG RUSSEGGER Ines is unbeatable, in particular in ice and mixed climbing. She is able to translate the skills gained in competitions to large rock faces. When we met in the North Wall of the Ortler I immediately liked her, she is a fun person to be around. What's the difference between the two of us? I only go into the mountains when I want to and because I enjoy it. To Ines, climbing is a profession.

KYRGYZSTAN I
KYZYL ASKER 2010

5.842 M

КЫЗЫЛ-АСКЕР

KYZYL ASKER – THE RED SOLDIER

»The vastness of the Thien Shan deeply impresses me. A day's walking – 16 km – lies between the base camp and the foot of the face.« *Ines Papert*

TAKING A LOOK at a photograph of Mount Kyzyl Asker, the 5.842 metre high »red soldier«, for the first time, I am simply overwhelmed. What a beautifully shaped mountain. It attracts me like magic. I can't get this picture out of my head. I even have a copy of the picture in my purse.
When Wolfgang Russegger, Thomas Senf and I are finally standing at the base of the wall, there is a mixture of anticipation, anxiety, hope, doubt and motivation in our thoughts, while we are amazed and full of respect, staring at the impressive and steep south-east face. What can we expect from Kyzyl Asker? What will it do with us? Will it let us celebrate on its peak?

»Arriving with the ›Ural‹ truck isn't possible. Too much fresh snow. We reach the base camp with a helicopter.« *Ines Papert*

»Massive water ice in the steep south east face. It's an absolute pleasure to be able to climb there.« *Ines Papert*

KAZAKSTAN KYRGYZSTAN

Bishkek

Songkul
Naryn
Kyzyl Asker

TAJIKISTAN CHINA

THE ROUTE THROUGH the 1.200 metre high, partly iced wall, which we selected for a possible first ascent, is very ambitious. The conditions are good. A promising, optimistic atmosphere surrounds us. The expectations are large. Even larger is the challenge which lies just in front of us. We are prepared to embrace this challenge.

Behind us lie crazy days. We abandon the original plan, to take a truck from Bishket, the capital of Kyrgyzstan, to Kookshai Too. The winter has arrived in the Kyrgis mountains of Thien Shan earlier than expected. The dirt road there is impassable. Do we fail, even before we've even seen the mountain we want to climb?

From the very first day, the Kyzyl Asker demands from us the ability to improvise and be flexible. At the same time, it overstains our budget. Then the only chance we have of getting to our base camp is by transporting 1,5 tons of luggage 400 kilometres by bus to Naryn. After that, we involuntarily board an army helicopter that would fly us to the mountains.

»Our first attempt ends after spending the night in a bivvy in the middle of the face. The weather changes suddenly. Thanks to the spindrift showers, the face offloads all of the fresh snow on top of us.« *Ines Papert*

THE HARDEST NIGHT OF MY LIFE

ON FOOT, we transport our material via the Kamovara glacier to the base camp. We have to march several times to the Advanced Base Camp (ABC), which is situated at 4.600 metres. The weather is bombastic and yet, although Wolfgang Russegger and I have become acclimatised, both of us are stuck in the tent with colds. After being forced to stop for several days, we risk an attempt at 4 am and start climbing up the wall. The weight of the backpacks, the strenuous mixed climbing with the solid ice, then the altitude – we are exhausted! Late in the day, we find a useful but not particularly comfortable spot to bivvy. Three small places to sit – that's the uncomfortable result of persistent work with our ice tools. After the meal, it begins to snow. We start to joke about a few spindrift showers that turn into heavy fresh snow downpours on us during the night. We are getting heavy snow, it's uncomfortable, windy, bitter cold. We remain silent, counting the hours, yearning for daylight. Without having to go into discussion, the message is clear for all of us: We have to abseil the very next morning.

After experiencing ten long days of bad weather in base camp, Charly Gabl offers us hope with his weather prediction. When the amount of fresh snow, which is blocking the wall, finally slides down, we make a new attempt. We climb a total of 17 hours in one go and reach a point which is just 200 metres below the summit. We are nearly there! We bivvy in a steep face. What follows, is the toughest night of my life. The announced bad weather front has arrived a day too early. Avalanches are moving down, temperatures are around minus 30 degrees and the stove isn't working. These a clear signs that we have to leave the face. Immediately! Any improvement in the weather? Not in sight! We abandon the expedition.

»Second attempt. We start at night and want to climb as high as possible, before the sun starts shining on the face, triggering off a dangerous avalanche.« *Ines Papert*

»After the hardest night of our lives spent in a bivvy. Thomas, Wolfi and I fail due to a fresh snowfall just 200 metres below the peak. We are exhausted and sad.« *Ines Papert*

»We set up a gear cache for next year. We'll be back!« *Ines Papert*

MY THOUGHTS ARE **WITH MY SON**

THE MAGIC AND AURA of this mountain outweighs the disappointment of having failed. We will pursue our goal and return in the forthcoming year. On the way home, I'm thinking about my son Manu, and I play with the idea of showing him Kyrgyzstan. The pristine nature and vastness of this country fascinates me. The cute children, who appear to be satisfied with their meagre life, touch my heart. I want to ride with Manu through the steppes, sleep in yurts and sample the freedom together. The journey through Kyrgyzstan should also show him how privileged our life in Germany is and also give him an insight into »my« life. The life of a professional mountain climber. Manu, as an eleven-year-old, is mature enough now to understand. He is also capable of reaching the base camp. He should view my mountain with his own eyes. Also, this journey, like any away from home, should also broaden his horizon. In my opinion, Kyrgyzstan is an ideal country to confront Manu with modesty, poverty and simple conditions. I feel safe and secure in Kyrgyzstan. What a beautiful country! Yes, my son has to travel there and see it! He'll be playing with children who cannot speak his language. However, he will still be able to understand them. Things will be different than at home. A lot more simple and sparse. He'll still love it. A concrete idea develops from a fleeting thought. My son will accompany me next year to Kyrgyzstan. I am really looking forward to this!

FACTS:
- ▲ BIVVY
- ROUTE : THE STILL TO BE CONQUERED SOUTHEAST WALL OF THE KYZYL ASKER
- HEIGHT OF FACE: 1200 M
- DIFFICULTY: WI6/M8

POSITION: N41°01'13.4" E077°21'27.2"

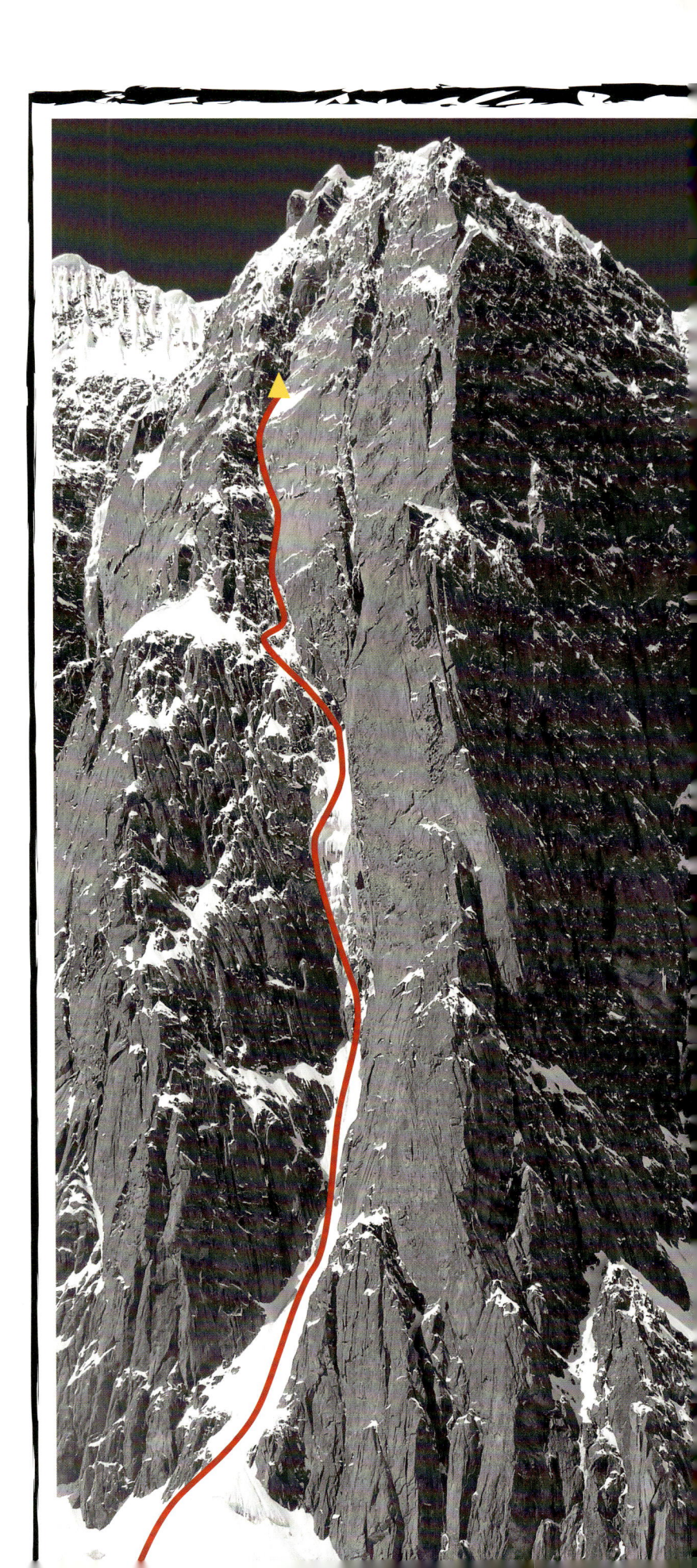

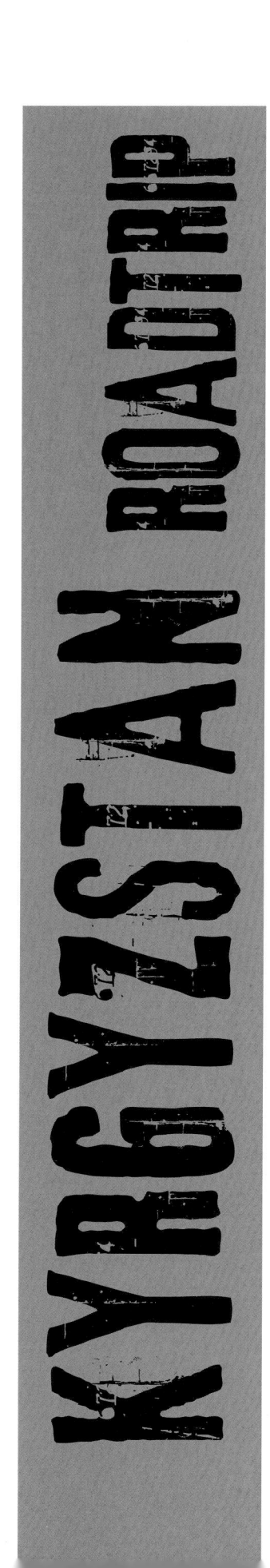

KYRGYZSTAN ROADTRIP

»A wonderful journey with my son Emanuel. On the way to the base camp, we stop off at the Song-Kul Lake and sleep with the nomads in their yurts.« *Ines Papert*

ENCHANTING DAYS
AT THE SONG-KUL LAKE

EMANUEL has actually come along. Two beautiful weeks lie ahead of us. On our tour of Kyrgyzstan, we sleep in yurts, in the living rooms of natives or in our tent. We undertake many walking tours in the mountains, enjoying charming days at the Song-Kul lake and riding through the steppes. Manu has his unicycle and football with him. Both of these simple objects overcome every language barrier. Children are simply able to understand each other. Playing.

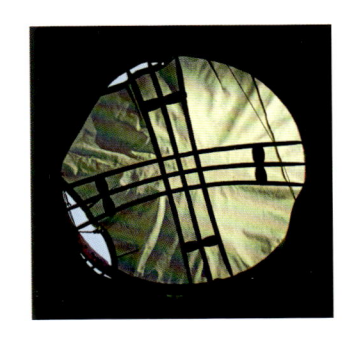

KYRGYZSTAN IS VAST AND QUIET

ALREADY ON THE north bank of Lake Issyk-Kul, there is no longer any tourism. We are after all in the Oxen valley on our own, completely isolated and thrilled. Kyrgyzstan is vast and quiet, rugged and sometimes wild. It is seldom idyllic and the countryside cannot be described as lovely. Unforgettably beautiful are the starlit, yet cold nights. At the Song-Kul lake, which lies at 3.500 metres, it's stormy and snowing in the middle of August! We see the traces of snow leopards, hordes of Marco Polo sheep and time and again, hundreds of horses. In Naryn, an old garrison town, we buy food at the market for the coming expedition. This is where our climbing partners Wolfgang Russegger and Charly Fritzer, who is standing in for Thomas Senf, meet up with us.

Peace, vastness, tranquility. Song-Kul Lake is paradise.

»We live like nomads. A ride through the steppe is part of the adventure.« *Ines Papert*

»Our truck ›Ural‹ gets stuck in the mud, 10 kilometres before reaching the base camp. A huge adventure for Emanuel, the first big hurdle for us alpinists.« *Ines Papert*

MY SON LEAVES AND I STAY

SHORTLY BEFORE WE reach base camp, our enthusiasm comes abruptly to an end. Our truck »Ural« starts to sink in the mud. Every further attempt to drag the vehicle out of the wet and muddy ground, makes it sink further into the mud. This is where the journey ends! That means: The expedition equipment has to be carried by foot to the base camp. When the decision stands, our driver Igor manages to excavate the lorry, which means that Manu will be able to travel home in time for the start of school. I find our parting extremely difficult. Normally I am the one who leaves my son behind. This time, it's the other way round. He leaves. I stay. The circumstances that I regularly put him under, by leaving, begins to really bother me.

KYRGYZSTAN II
KYZYL ASKER 2011

»Illness and the motivation problems arising from it burden the whole team. I had a feeling that we were going to fail. Yet I didn't really want to believe it.« *Ines Papert*

HOPELESS
THE MORALE HITS ROCK BOTTOM

IT ONLY TAKES a couple of days before the pleasant anticipation of climbing Kyzyl Asker disappears. Will we make it this time? We are well prepared. Our expectations are gigantic. Sadly however, Charly und Wolfgang become ill and their recuperation at 4.000 metres is very slow. We are enjoying excellent weather and are condemned to idleness. After a very long delay, we begin transporting the material to the ABC. The morale within the team is tense and is close to tilting. Nobody is to blame and yet each one of us has in her or his own way contributed to the misery. I have to thank my impatience that we want to use a period of good weather to start climbing the face. Maybe this is too early? Charly isn't really fit enough yet. Also, the threat of ice rocks falling due to warm temperatures has to be taken into consideration. We decide to abseil from the place where we pitched our bivvy at 5.300 metres in height. Demotivation creeps in on the quiet. We hardly speak to one another. The morale in the team hits rock bottom. I begin to feel that there is no point, trying to start another attempt. I'm having difficulty accepting this. I have given way to this mountain. I have adjusted my life and my training for two whole years to conquer it. Is that all I'm going to get out of it?

A QUANTUM OF **SOLACE**

BEFORE I DO finally head for home, accompanied by Wolfgang Russegger, I succeed at doing the first complete climb of the »Great Walls of China« taking a new route, yet I am far from being satisfied.
Therefore we baptize out 600 m long ice/mixed route »A Quantum of Solace«. Rating M7/WI7.
Before climbing into the truck that picks us up, I turn around one more time, to look for the last time at »my« mountain. Then, I actually begin to smile. I continue to carry this image with me. I know that I will be back here again. Sometime. Despite two failed attempts. This mountain still has a grip on me and it won't let go.

This small piece of paper was the catalyst for the idea of travelling to the Kyzyl Asker.

»Under difficult circumstances, yet another, and this time adesperate, attempt at the Kyzyl Asker, fails. At the end Wolfi and I manage the first complete climb of the Great Walls of China, 5.100 metres.« *Ines Papert*

A QUANTUM OF SOLACE | FIRST ASCENT
HEIGHT OF FACE: 600 M | ABO, WI7+ | M7

POSITION: 29°45'45''N 126°38'E

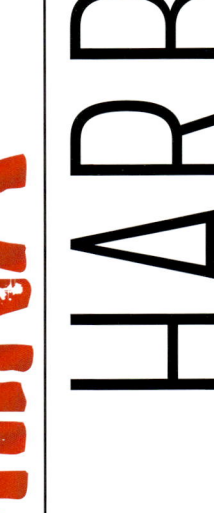

CHINA
HARBIN

I AM ON A SKIING TRIP when a friend of mine, Johanna Stöckl, who is a journalist, calls me. She rambles on about this spectacular ice festival in China and asks me if I would consider going there to climb. It's all Greek to me. In the evening, I click a link on my computer, which includes photographs. I am speechless. A whole city, built out of ice.

FIRST ASCENTS UP TO 18 M HEIGHT OF WALL AND WI6

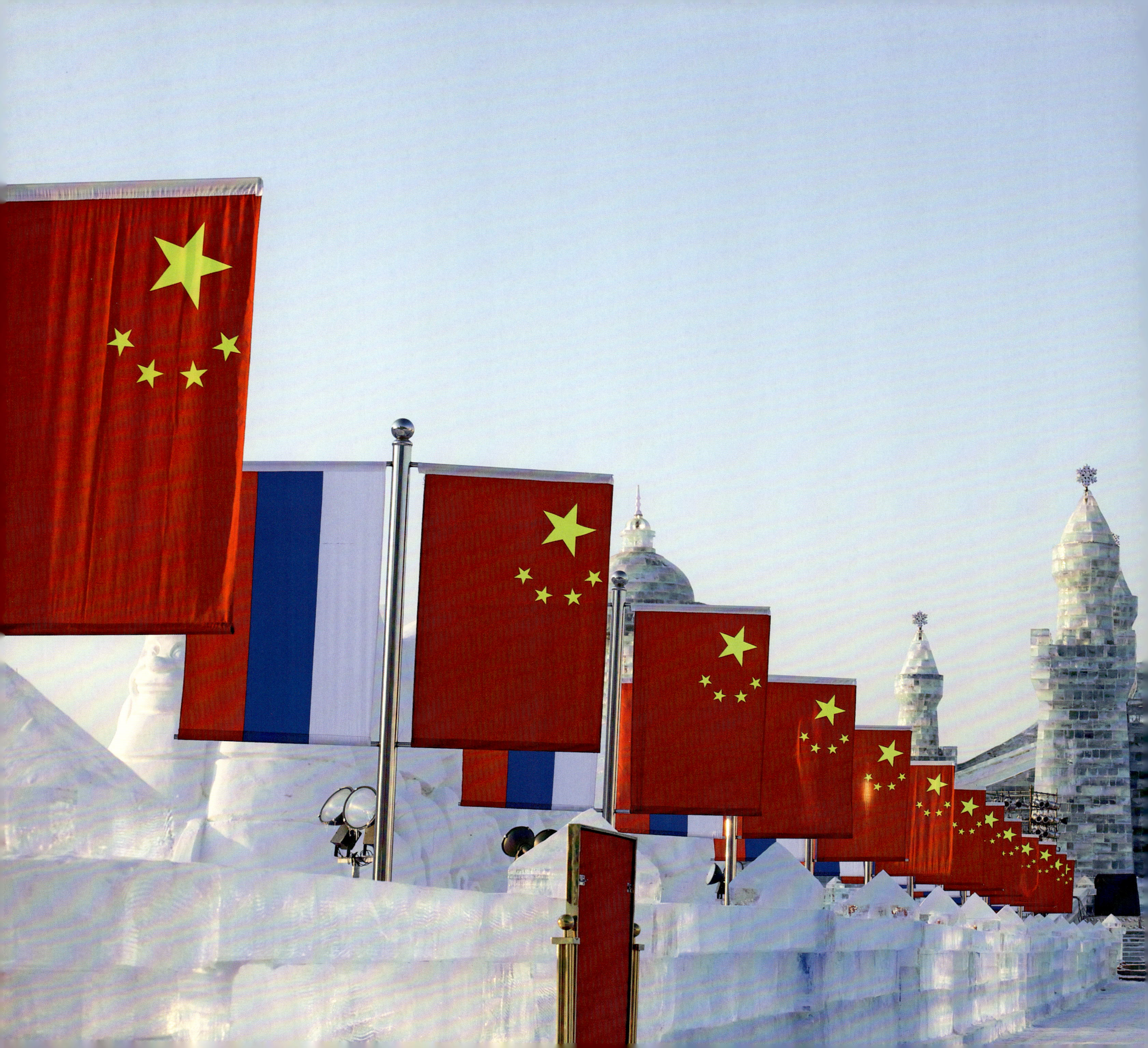

IT'S NOT ONLY the pictures that fascinate me. But also the fact that, despite the extreme temperatures that Harbin experiences in winter – the thermometer is constantly below minus 20 degrees Celsius – it impresses me, that they still want to celebrate by having a festival. I discover that we have a lot in common. I like the coldness. I love the ice. It's my medium. I really feel at home with this atmosphere. I interpret the Harbin ice spectacle as a song of praise to transitoriness, and I decide, together with Johanna, Franz and Tischi, to travel to Harbin. We are curious and pursue from now on the daring idea, that I will climb the spectacular buildings there that are made of ice. The communication with China, as we expected, doesn't run quite according to plan. When I find out that there never has been such a request like this one before, I start to jubilate. However, I am not yet aware of the bureaucratic barriers awaiting us ahead.

»To receive the official invitation from the city of Harbin, took a fair bit of work.« *Ines Papert*

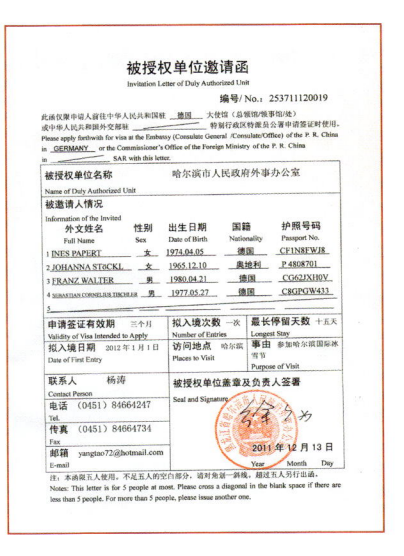

ONE YEAR LATER, we get to see the city made of ice. Andes Kang Hua, a mountain guide from Peking, is my belay partner. Despite the shyness he showed in the beginning, he starts to thaw quickly in frosty Harbin. We spend some exciting days in this city with its nine million inhabitants. I get to climb nearly every building. When the lights go on at night, the ice city becomes colourful and gaudy. My night sessions are well watched. Hundreds of people are cheering for me when I'm climbing. Overwhelming. With my activities, which from a sporting point of view, are not challenging – they are more cultural, artistic projects – I connect with the people and they connect with me. The Lord Mayor of Harbin asks me to give a speech at an international conference. I accept his invitation.

»I have to admit, climbing at night becomes a cute and colorful highlight of our tour.« *Ines Papert*

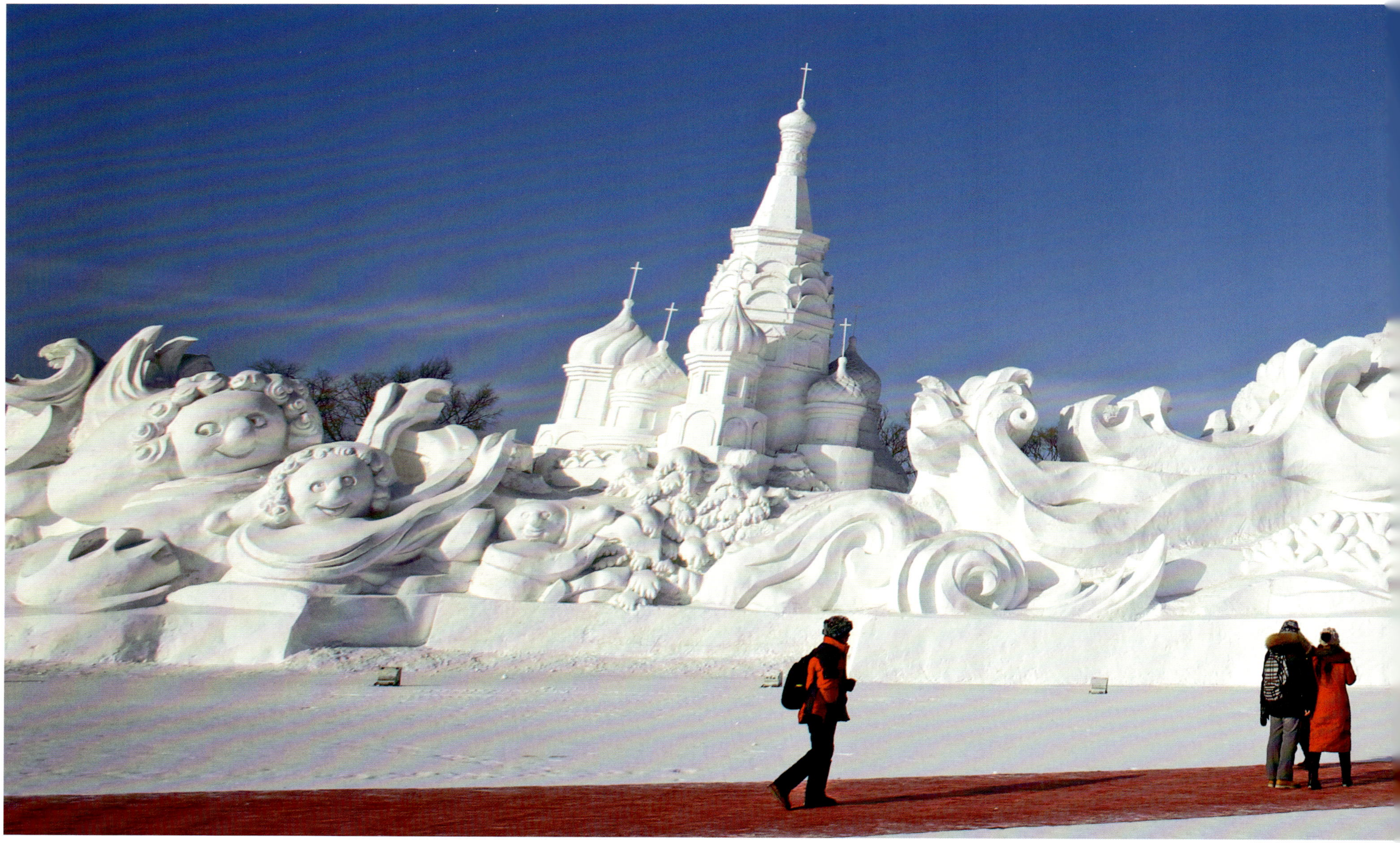

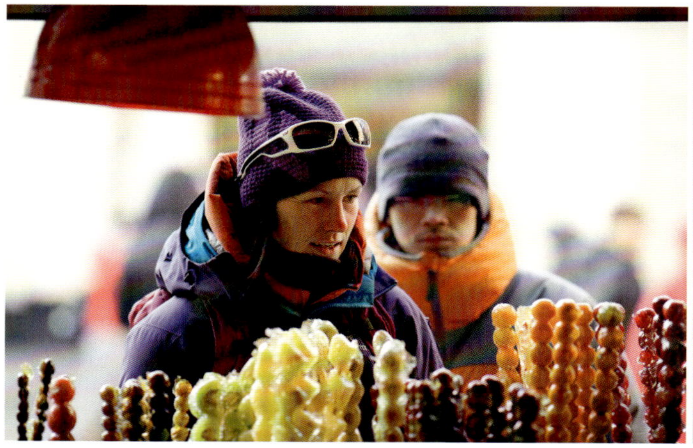

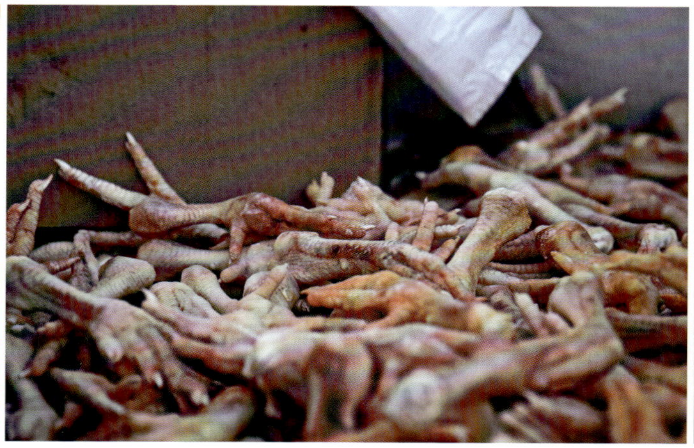

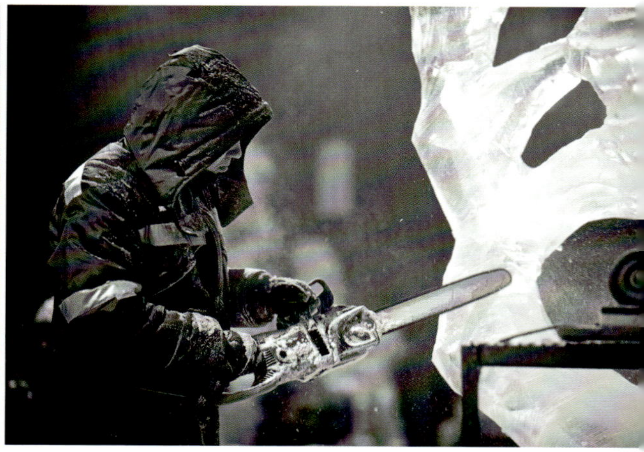

»When viewing the gigantic sculptures made of snow, we really are speechless.« *Ines Papert*

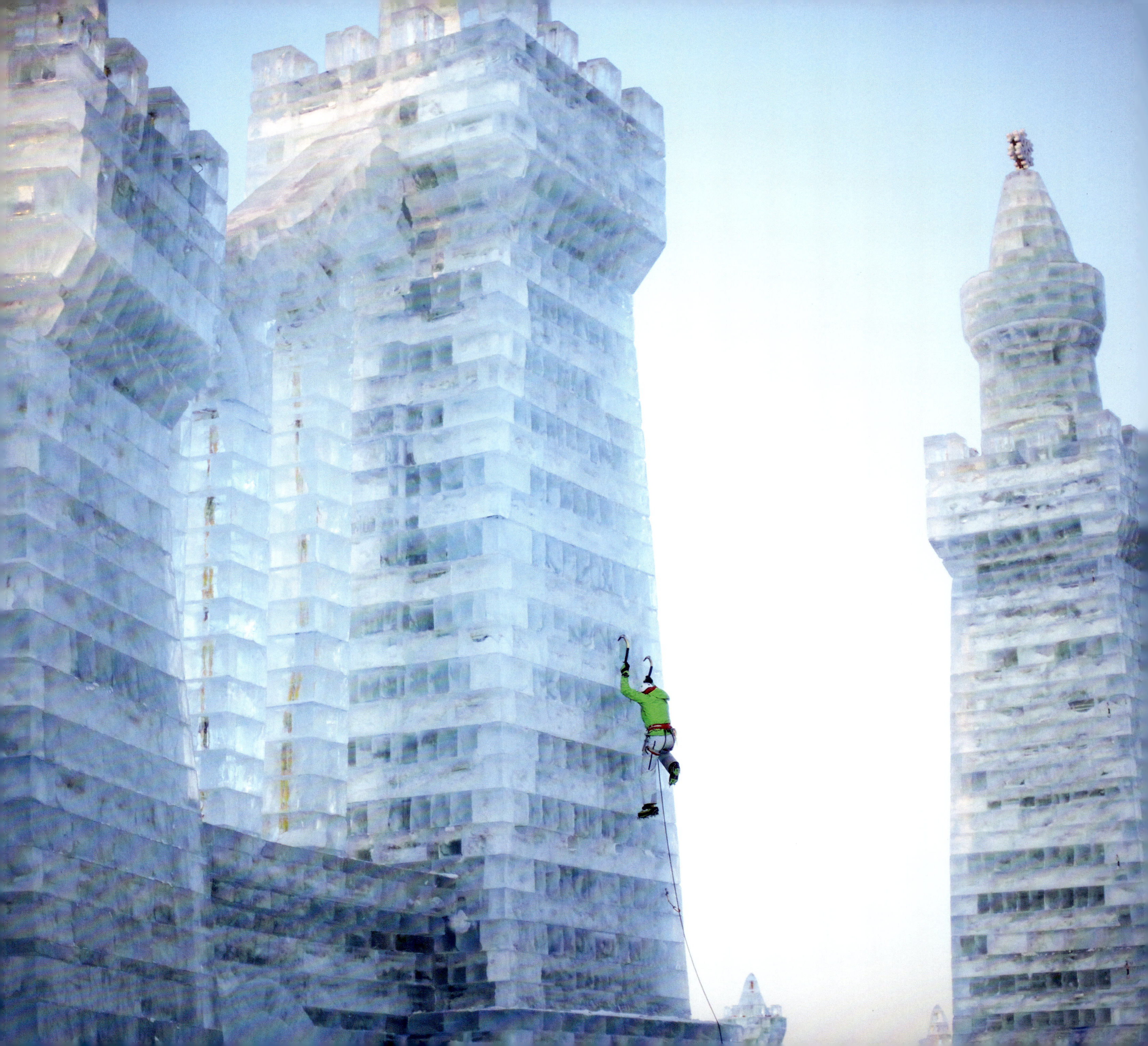

»We have huge respect for the winter swimmers in Harbin.« *Ines Papert*

SINCE 1985, Harbin organises an annual international ice and snow festival. In an area as large as 16 football fields, more than 12.000 workers develop a wonder world out of ice. The huge towers, impressive palaces, bridges, ice slides and spectacular cathedrals are built from single blocks or bricks of ice. These are gained from the frozen Songhua River that splits the city into a north and south shore. Also Sun-Island, Harbins summer recreation park, is transformed in the winter months due to the staging of the festival into the so-called Snow-World, where international snow artists create gigantic sculptures from snow.
What do I take with me from Harbin? A lot of fantastic experiences many touching encounters. I found the Chinese hospitality deeply impressive. I make friends with Andes, who told me a lot about his mountains in China. Maybe in the near future, we will start out on ar expedition together.

NORWAY
ROMSDALEN

»Our lodge, lying picturesque on the Sunndalenfjord in the Romsdalen region.« *Ines Papert*

»We forget the coldness of the face in the wood-burning Jacuzzi.« *Ines Papert*

INTENSIVE EXPERIENCE often finish up in a tavern and sometimes they even begin there. In the late autumn, my climbing colleague Kurt Astner and I, after spending a magnificent day climbing in the Ziller valley, are sitting inside Gasthaus Karlsteg, an inn in a village called Ginzling in Austria. At the table next to us, Rudi Hauser and Lukas Seiwand are eagerly waffling on about their forthcoming ice climbing trip in February to Norway. Being curious, we are listening to them. Openly and warmly, as Austrians usually are, they spontaneously ask us, if we'd also fancy coming along, to discover new routes in a seemingly wonderful area.

»A fisherman takes us to the other side of the fjord in his boat, allowing us to climb the unspoiled waterfall.« *Ines Papert*

DØREN SKAL VÆRE LÅST

THE TWO AUSTRIANS, Rudi Hauser and Lukas Seiwald, flew via Amsterdam. Kurt Astner and Emanuele Ciullo came from Italy, joined by the Swiss photographer Thomas Senf, cameraman Scott Milton from Canada, and finally, my humble self. We all landed in Trondheim. We took a hire car and drove along the Norwegian west coast. There, the fjords drag themselves as steep gorges going deep into the countryside. Enormous rock faces have formed on both the left and the right, several hundred metres high. Breathtaking! We stayed in a very comfortable base camp, the so-called »Salmon lodge«. At this stage there is an overwhelming anticipation and motivation to get going.

NORWAY

Romsdalen
Trondheim
Oslo
SWEDEN
FINLAND
RUSSIA

I AM THE ONLY woman in a team which includes six men. Not exactly what you would call the classical role allocation! On the very first day, our chef Rudi buys a decent fillet knife and »pimps up« our kitchen equipment. When we arrive back at the base after completing a successful climb, within minutes, our living room transforms into a specialized climbing store. Mind you, the range of goods looks somewhat chaotic. We all have to tidy up together. Rudi, still wearing his climbing gear, divides the tasks amongst us. Collecting the wood, drying the laundry, heating up the Jacuzzi, boiling the water, cooling the beer.

Climbing with a terrific deep view of the Eikesfjord.

FIRST ASCENT
SEA GULL JONATHAN | WI6
HEIGHT OF THE WALL: 250 M | PAPERT/SEIWALD/MILTON

FURTHER FIRST ASCENTS BESIDE THOSE ALREADY REFERRED TO:

SURPRICE | WI6+/M8 | CLEAN | 350 M | LITLDALEN SUNNDALSØRA | PAPERT/SENF

DRIVA HELLE FOSSEN | CLEAN | WI6 | 250 M | ERESFJORD | HAUSER/ASTNER

QUATTRO NAZIONI | WI6/M9/A1 | 1 BOLT IN THE ROUTE | 500 M | EIKESDAL LEFT SIDE OF THE VALLEY | PAPERT/SENF/CIULLO/SEIWALD

ULTIMATE RUSH | WI7+/8- | CLEAN | 150 M | AMOTAN | TO THE LEFT BESIDE THE LARGE WATERFALL | HAUSER/ASTNER

POSITION: 62°40'N 8°37'E

THE FIRST DAYS climbing prove to be relatively difficult. There is very little information available about this area. Even on the internet, little or nothing can be found about climbing here. The Norwegian climbers are a committed group who don't broadcast their successes. To us, this initially means: We will start, where our eyes can predict a very good route. Unaware, whether or not we'll have to repeat a route or start a first ascent. Curiously enough, our landlady Perly, who lives with her family next door to us, will become the key to our success. She is not only a true organisational genius. She is also quite active on Facebook and amongst other things, she is good friends with the climbing legend Björn Magne Overas. Like many Norwegian sportspeople, he also works offshore on one of the oil platforms and makes use of the long breaks in between his work assignments by remaining active as a climber. In short notice, he comes to visit us and shows us amazing pictures, showering us with information. As early as the Eighties, he planned a passage with a bivvy of the legendary »Mardalsfossen«. Unfortunately, the handle of his ice axe broke, which was made of bamboo. Today, in his mid-fifties, Björn still climbs, obviously with better equipment than when he started out. Thanks to his help, we have found out which routes are virginal and the routes we – unsuspectingly – have already climbed for the first time.

Rudi Hauser with Kurt Astner on the new route »Offshore« WI7+/8-.

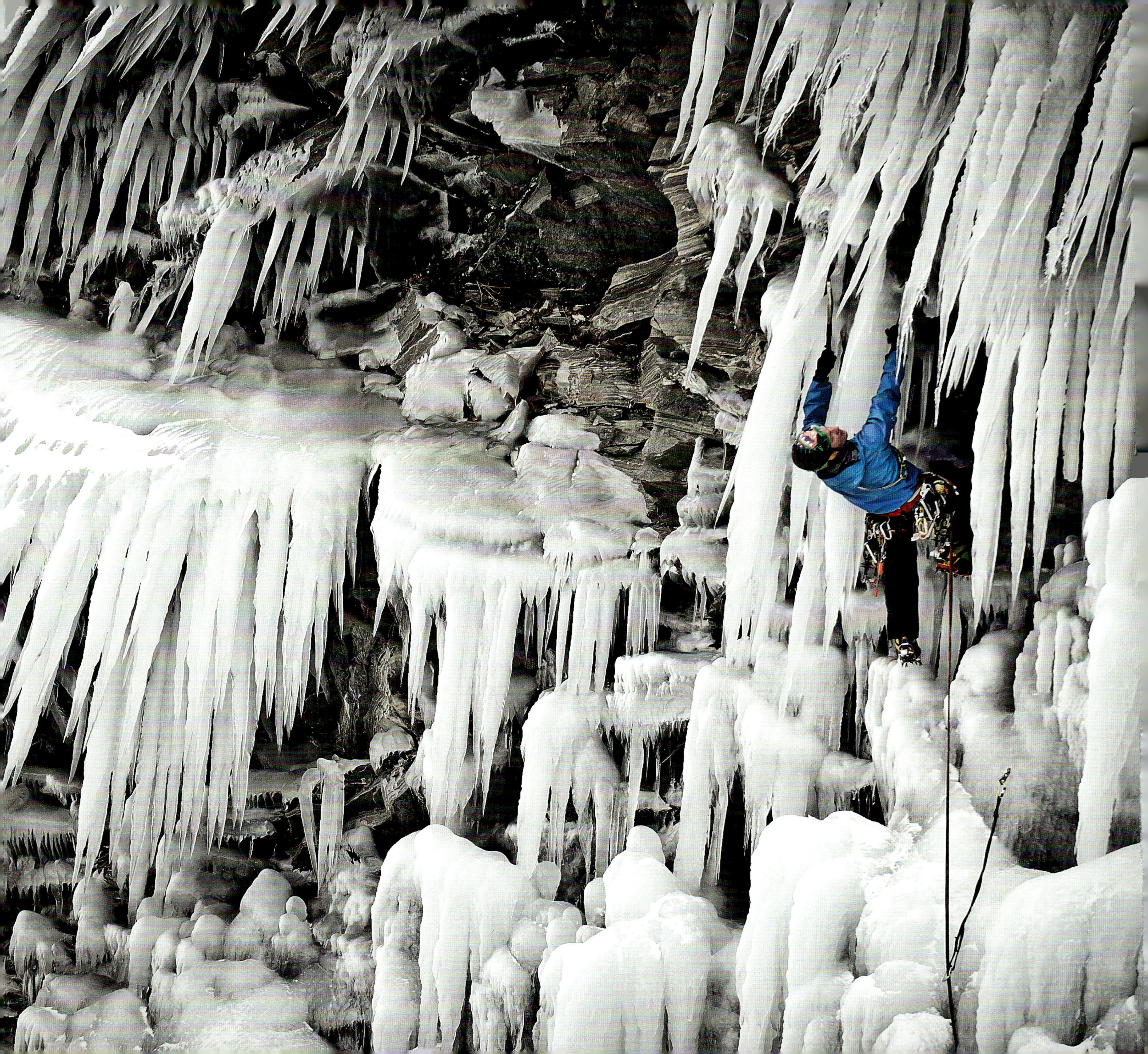

Ines in »Quattro Nazioni«/Eikesdal.

FIFTY DOLLAR 50 $ KING CRAB | M10 WI5+ | 5 BOLTS IN THE ROUTE, 300 M, IN EIKESDAL | YELLOW WATERFALL AT THE END OF THE VALLEY | PAPERT/SENF/MILTON

I EXPERIENCED my personal highlight when climbing together with Lukas and Scott. We sail in a fishing boat from Eisvag across the Eresfjord to the steep face on the opposite side. There, high about the fjord, we are able to conquer »Sea Gull Jonathan«, while Rudi, Kurt and Senfi climb »Offshore«. Two routes parallel to each other, which no person before us has ever climbed. An extraordinary group adventure of a special kind. In the evening, sitting in a Jacuzzi, I view a Northern Light for the very first time. What a pleasant moment, where everything seems to be perfect!

ARCTIC
BAFFIN ISLAND | MOUNT ASGARD

2.015 M

POSITION: 66°40'20''N 65°16'28''W

»In the summer of 2012, I head off, together with Jon Walsh and Joshua Lavigne, to the northeastern part of Baffin Island, the fifth largest island on the planet.« *Ines Papert*

142

WHEREAS ONE CAN rely on pleasant and short slopes in the Big Wall Mekka Yosemite Valley, one has to reserve a lot more time for the great walls on Baffin Island. The reward: a real adventure in a remote and secluded region. Passing through Iqualuit, we reach the town of Pangnirtung, with its 1.500 inhabitants. From there, we take a fisherboat travelling 30 kilometres across the fjord, before continuing on foot with a lot of luggage across the moraine countryside towards Mount Asgard, along the Weasel Valley in the Auyuittuq National Park. I have a lot of respect for the demanding, freezing glacial streams that we have to conquer.

Arrival at Summit Lake at the end of the second day stage. Looking back at Weasel Valley. Gigantic cliffs piled up on both sides of the valley. We leave Mount Thor and Mount Breidalvik behind us. Our ultimate destination, Mount Asgard, has concealed itself for a long time.

BAFFIN ISLAND

Auyuittuq-National Park

Mt Asgard
Pangnirtung

Iqaluit

CANADA

BAFFIN ISLAND'S LANDSCAPE is simply unique. Scant, without any trees and with the exception of a couple of weeks during the year, where the fjords are free of ice, it's an area hostile to humans. Steep cliffs, as far as the eye can see. One can get lost in this almost endless glacier region. Quiet. Very beautiful. Timeless. Since the sun doesn't sink during the summer months, we have daylight around the clock. My headlamp, a compulsory tool in my backpack, isn't required for this adventure. After a three day foot march, we reach the Turner glacier at the foot of Mount Asgard and set up our base camp. The march was troublesome so far. When crossing the numerous glacial streams, with the force of the water, one has to be extremely careful. This is no place for slipping up. This does have one advantage of course: Endless amounts of drinking water of the highest quality is available. In 2008, when Jon Walsh was in this region climbing several peaks, he had his eyes on the northwest wall of Mount Asgard. Then, the only thing that prevented him from tackling it, was the huge amount of snow at the time.

145

MOUNT LOKI | 1.920 M

TO WARM-UP and get used to each other as a team, we climb Mount Loki, Baffin's »Matterhorn«. Enjoying ideal conditions, we climb the route of a New Zealand team through the 700 metre high south pillar and reach the peak around midnight. We are probably the first to complete a free ascent of this route. A good enough reason to be satisfied. Time and again, our view wanders across to Mount Asgard. Was this the right decision to take? Maybe taking advantage of the good weather, we should have climbed our original aim, Mount Asgard? Doubtful.

Perfect hand and finger cracks alternate while climbing chimneys. Being able to experience the pure pleasure of climbing at a moderate level. Not until we reach the headwall, does the wall begin to become steep.

»We are probably the first ones to achieve the free ascent of the New Zealand route.« *Ines Papert*

SOUTH BUTTRESS | 5.10+

HEIGHT OF FACE: 700 M

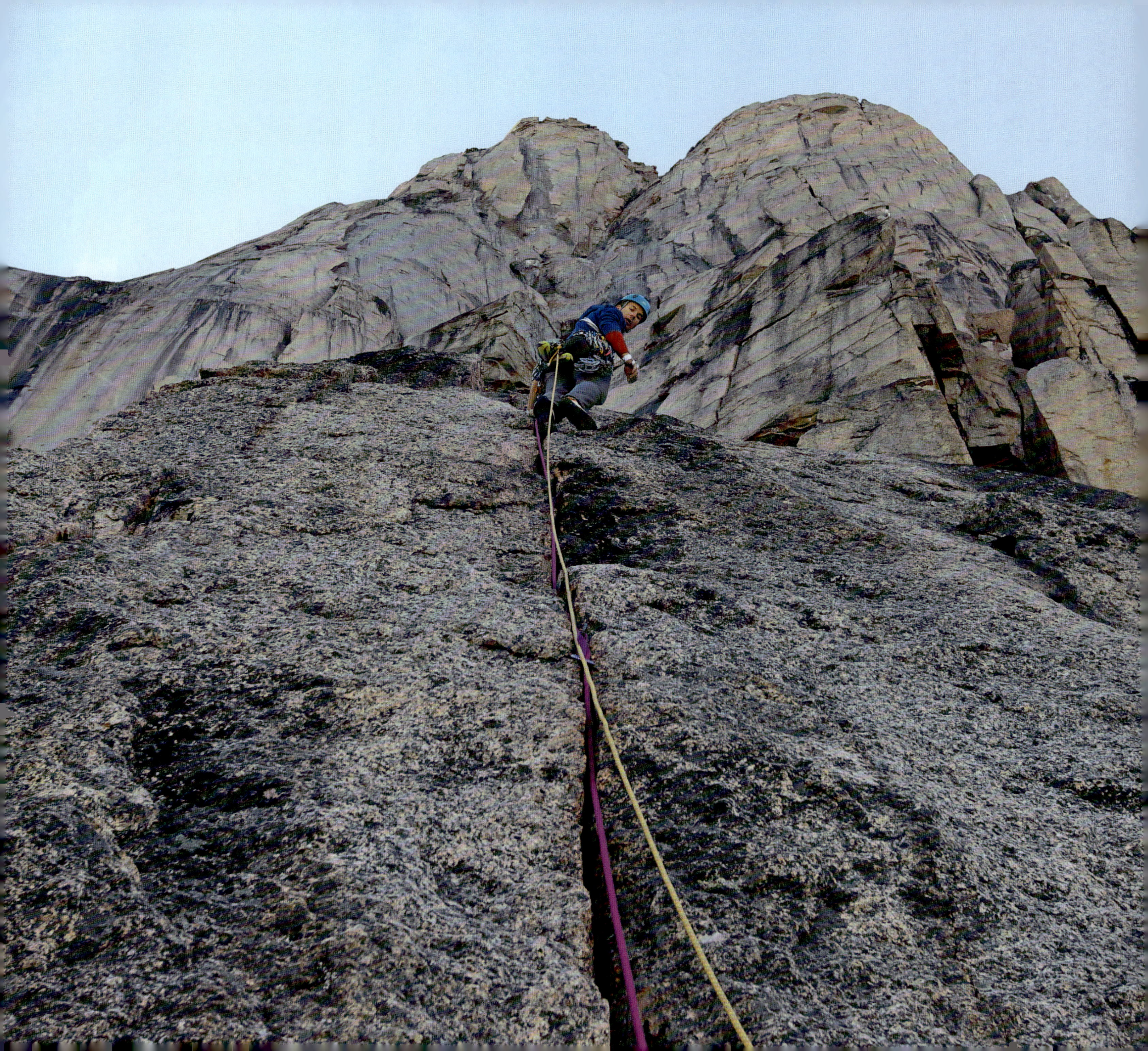

»We've decided to take a direct route on Mount Asgard, starting at the big toe at the base. For the fun of it, we are calling it the ›seated start‹.« *Ines Papert*

»OUR« MOUNTAIN with its distinctive, two cylinder steeple silhouette is called after Asgard, the home of the Gods in Nordic mythology. Its 1.200 metre high rock face is regarded as one of the steepest and tallest in the world. What do we intend doing? The first ascent of the north west wall of the South Towers, the one on the right side of both plateau peaks. In order to be fast and efficient, we decide on the following strategy: Three rope lengths will be lead in one piece, either by Jon, Josh or me. One climber will follow using jumars on a rope going up and pulling the haulbag along. One further person will follow as usual with the somewhat lighter backpack. We commence at four o'clock and already reach the middle of the wall during the morning. Its our aim not to use any bolts. In the afternoon, falling rocks could be dangerous. We try to side step to the right, yet we can't find any continuous crack system. Back we go. Bivvy under a protective rock shelter. We have to wait until the following morning for cooler temperatures.

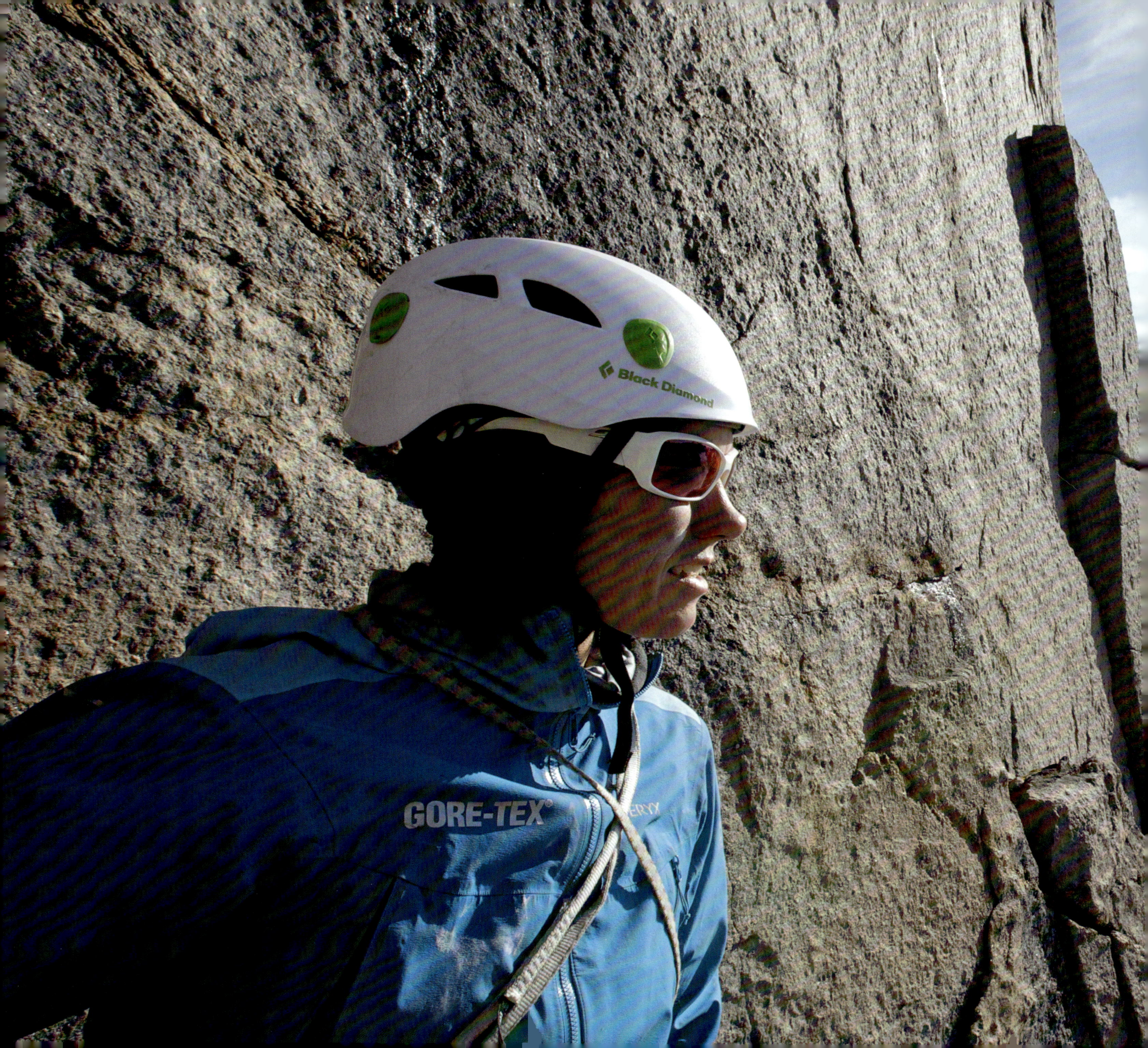
Black Diamond
GORE-TEX

»For just a moment, I enjoy the breathtaking view of the Turner glacier. We are situated in the middle of a heavenly, yet weird landscape.« *Ines Papert*

»I am grateful for every rope length in the leading climb. Then, I don't have to drag the cumbersome backpack with me.« *Ines Papert*

THE OUTCOME OF the climatic change can be seen. Whole rocks – retained for centuries thanks to permafrost – loosen up from the mountain due to the increasing temperatures during the summer months. I feel queasy. I am slightly nervous. That's why I am extra careful climbing towards the peak. Thankfully, the quality of the cliff is a lot better further up.

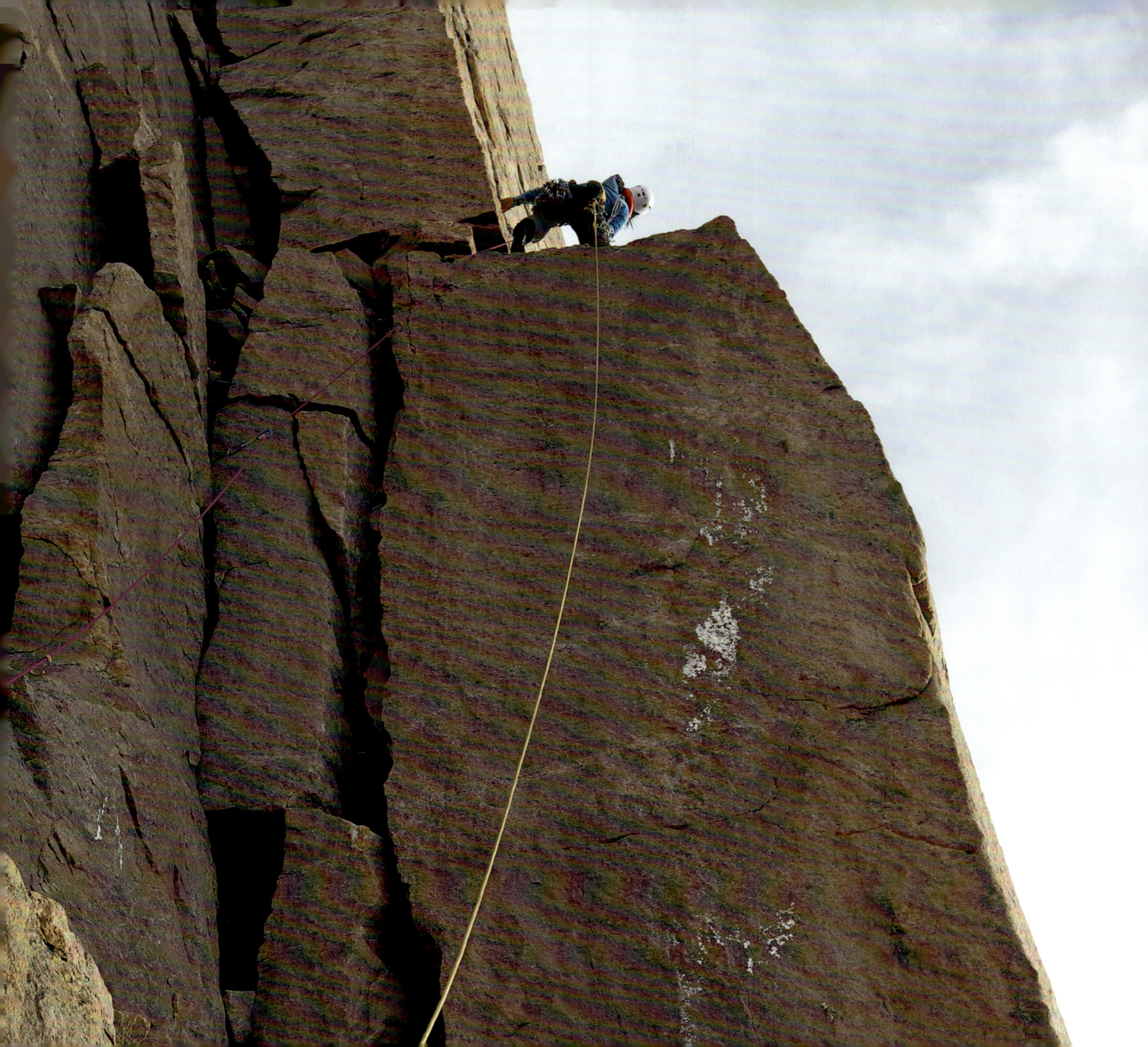

The 16th wire length, a 100 metre Off-With 5.11+, becomes climbing technically, the key section.

AS WE ARE underway in alpine style, we are carrying the minimum amount of luggage and have few provisions with us. This should enable us to reach the peak on the second day. For the twentieth time, we are having Pat Thai to eat, even here on the wall. At the last minute, all Jon was able to come up with were rice dishes. A 100 metre long, very wide Off-With (body crack) becomes the actual key section in the second part of the wall. To overcome it in complete exposure, is nerve-racking and rather hard graft. We've only got one large camelot with us. It's my turn on the lead climb and I fight my way upwards. The preparation as a team, training on Mount Lok, has paid off. I've been with Jon Walsh on several tours already. I only got to know Josh here. The team work is functioning excellently.

MOUNT ASGARD | NORTHWEST FACE

HEIGHT OF FACE: 1.200 M | FIRST ASCENT IN ALPINE STYLE, 3 DAYS

JUST BELOW the peak, there is a radical change in the weather. An emerging storm makes our last two rope lengths difficult and we have no visibility on the peak. With the exception of a frozen chimney and due to strong rain, a wet tension on the exit length, we are able to climb everything onsight. However, the joy is somewhat limited, then with worsening conditions, we are getting very worried. There's no way that we can bivvy on the peak. It's too windy. Bitter cold. We have to get off the mountain. Thanks to the fog, we can't find the way down through the south side of Mount Asgard. We have to climb down through the plate-like rugged terrain, which is dangerously wet and slippy, before staying here in a bivvy. Ludicrous: We've nothing left to drink. Even though it's raining, we are dying of thirst. It's not raining strong enough to be able to catch enough water.

SENSORY OVERLOAD 5.11+
GEAR: CAMELOTS/CHOCKS

BY THE TIME we arrive back at our camp, we've been away for 60 hours. After the unexpectedly quick success on Mount Asgard, it is our plan on the way back through Weasel Valley, to maybe try one or the other walls. While passing thought Summit Lake, Jon receives the very sad news of the bereavement of his father. Of course, we'll accompany him on his way back. However, we have to be fast. That's why we'll leave some material behind, which will be picked up by skidoo in the winter. Off we go on an 18 hour walk back to the fjord, which we do in one go. Jon makes it back home in time for the funeral.

HENCE, my book finishes with a successful yet sad chapter which I didn't originally plan. Life tends to write it's own stories. The expedition to Baffin Island was up to now, my most intensive one. From the first day in the wilderness, we could hear and see every sign of nature, regardless of its size. For example, protecting us from polar bears or rocks that were threatening to fall. We were fully alert and highly concentrated. Baffin gave us on this beautiful island 100 % attentiveness from the first to the very last step. The original reason for travelling there, was the climbing. Yet, what is really important, is the other experiences we had during this expedition. For me, the success we achieved was only a fraction of the total all-round experience we had on this important journey.

My son Manu will be flying into Canada with my partner Wolfi in a few days. It is while visiting friends, following this expedition, where I am now, sitting down and finishing the last lines for this book. A family holiday is on the horizon. You can't imagine how much I am looking forward to seeing my loved ones!

For more than ten years, our partnership with Ines Papert has been based on trust and respect. A relationship that is characterised by the joint push for new experiences. Similar to an expedition, there are often unexpected challenges that need to be mastered and new soil that needs to be broken when developing ever better materials. This is why Ines Papert's extreme activities in mountainous terrain are both valuable and important for the further development of our products. Today and in future.

Bibliographical information of the German National Library (DNB)
The German National Library lists this publication in the German National Bobliography; detailed bibliographic data can be retrieved in the Internet via http://dnb.d-nb.de.

1st edition
ISBN 978-3-7688-3561-9
© by Delius Klasing & Co. KG, Bielefeld (Germany)

COVER DESIGN | isar 12 grafik, design, illustrationen | Isabella Flemisch | g24 | wehrs graphik design werbung | Hubert Wehrs

LAYOUT | isar 12 grafik, design, illustrationen | Isabella Flemisch

TEXT | Johanna Stöckl

PHOTO CREDITS | **FRONT COVER**: Cory Richards (t.), Thomas Senf | visualimpact.ch (b.) | **BACK COVER**: Thomas Senf | visualimpact.ch (t.), Keith Ladzinski (b.) | **BACK FLAP**: Franz Walter | **CONTENT**: Heinz Aemmer | visualimpact.ch: 28–35, 91 (t. r.), 94 (b.) | Chris Atkinson: 69 (b. l.), 69 (b. r.) 70/71, 73/74, 92 (t. r.) | Greg Boswell: 92 (b. c.) | Andrew Burr: S. 91 (b. r.) | Rainer Eder | visualimpact.ch: 4/5, 10, 11 (b. l., r.), 12, 16 (b.), 17 (b. l., b. r.) | Audrey Gariepy: 57 (r.) | Hansi Heckmair: 17 (t.) | Hans Hornberger: 26/27, 78 (b. l.), 79–83, 85–89, 92 (b. r.) | Anita Kolar: 31 (b. l.), 34 (t. l.) | Eberhard Köpf: 57 (b.) | Frank Kretschmann: 8/9 | Wolfgang Kurz: 110 (t.) | Keith Ladzinski: 6, 18–23 | Joshua Lavigne: 146 (t. l.), 150–152, 158 (t. l.) | Ines Papert: 56, 76 (t., b.), 77, 106 (b. r.), 107, 114/115 | Ian Parnell: 78 (b. r.), 78/79, 84 (b. r.) | Marc Piché: 66–69, 72, 75, 96 (t. l.) | Cory Richards: 6, 50–53, 55, 57 (l.), 58/59, 60–65, 91 (b. l.), 93 (t. l.), 95 (t. l.) | Thomas Senf | visualimpact.ch: 6, 13–15, 24/25, 92 (b. l.), 95 (b. r.), 96 (b. c.), 97 (t. l.), 99, 101/102, 103 (l.), 104/105, 106 (l., t. r., c. l., c.., c. r.), 116/117, 128–139 | Lisi Steurer: 68 (b. l.), 68 (b. r.) | Johanna Stöckl: 122 (b. r.), 123 (b. l.) | Jost von Allmen | visualimpact.ch: 16 (t.) | Jon Walsh: S. 36–49, 95 (t. r.), 140–149, 153–159 | Franz Walter | visualimpact.ch: 90, 91 (t. l.), 93 (b. l.), 96 (b. r.), 98–101, 103 (r.), 108–113, 118/119, 121–127 | Archiv Hari Berger: 93 (b. r.) | Archiv Moni Kallsperger: 97 (t. r.) | Archiv Joshua Lavigne: S. 95 (b. l.) | Archiv Dave MacLeod: S. 93 (t. r.) | Archiv Ines Papert: S. 11 (t. l.) | Archiv Ian Parnell: S. 94 (t. l.) | Archiv Marc Piché: S. 96 (b. l.) | Archiv Wolfgang Russegger: S. 97 (b. r.) | Archiv Liv Sansoz: S. 96 (t. r.) | Archiv Johanna Stöckl: S. 94 (t. r.) | Archiv Simon Yearsley: S. 97 (b. l.)

CONCEPT AND ADVISE | Petra Thaller | Ideenschmiede Berg

EDITING AND FINAL ARTWORK | Stefanie Baiter

LITHOGRAPHY | digital | data | medien, Bad Oeynhausen

PRINTING | Kunst- und Werbedruck, Bad Oeynhausen

Printed in Germany 2012
All rights reserved! The work may neither be entirely nor partially reproduced, transmitted or copied – such as manually or by means of electronic and mechanical systems, including photocopying, tape recording and data storage – without explicit permission of the publisher.

DELIUS KLASING VERLAG
Siekerwall 21, D-33602 Bielefeld
Tel.: +49 (0)521/559-0; fax: +49 (0)559115
E-mail: info@delius-klasing.de
www.delius-klasing.de

BAFFIN ISLAND

CIRQUE OF THE UNCLIMBABLES

CANADA

ICEFALL BROOK CANYON